# TEACHING WITH TABLETS

# TEACHING WITH TABLETS

#HELEN CALDWELL #JAMES BIRD

Los Angeles | London | New Delhi
Singapore | Washington DC

Learning Matters
An imprint of SAGE Publications Ltd
1 Oliver's Yard
55 City Road
London EC1Y 1SP

SAGE Publications Inc.
2455 Teller Road
Thousand Oaks, California 91320

SAGE Publications India Pvt Ltd
B 1/I 1 Mohan Cooperative Industrial Area
Mathura Road
New Delhi 110 044

SAGE Publications Asia-Pacific Pte Ltd
3 Church Street
#10-04 Samsung Hub
Singapore 049483

Editor: Amy Thornton
Development editor: Geoff Barker
Production controller: Chris Marke
Project management: Swales & Willis Ltd, Exeter,
Devon
Marketing manager: Lorna Patkai
Cover design: Wendy Scott
Typeset by: C&M Digitals (P) Ltd, Chennai, India
Printed and bound in Great Britain by: Henry Ling
Limited at The Dorset Press, Dorchester, DT1 1HD

**Library of Congress Control Number: 2014958162**

**British Library Cataloguing in Publication Data**

A catalogue record for this book is available from
the British Library

MIX
Paper from
responsible sources
FSC
www.fsc.org   FSC™ C013985

ISBN: 978-1-4739-0678-5
ISBN: 978-1-4739-0679-2 (pbk)

# Contents

# The authors

**Helen Caldwell** is the curriculum lead for Primary Computing in Teacher Education at the University of Northampton. Her teaching covers the use of technology across primary subjects, implementing the computing curriculum and assistive technologies for SEN. She provides CPD (Continuing Professional Development) for teachers and Initial Teacher Trainees across these areas, and her research focuses on the effective use of mobile devices in primary classrooms.

**James Bird** works within the School of Education at Oxford Brookes University. His research, CPD and consultancy work includes a focus on learning, pedagogy and technology. He combines work as a primary teacher trainer alongside work as a school improvement professional within a multi-academy trust, which also includes use of technology to enhance and support learning.

**Yasemin Allsop** worked as an ICT Coordinator in primary schools in London for almost ten years. She is currently employed as Senior Lecturer in Primary Computing and ICT at Manchester Metropolitan University. She has an MA ICT in Education from the London Knowledge Lab, University of London. She is also an MPhil/PhD student at Goldsmiths, University of London, focusing on children's thinking, learning and metacognition when designing digital games. She is the editor of an online magazine called *ICT in Practice* where educators from around the world share their experiences of using technology in education.

**David Andrews** specialises in delivering 'outstanding' lessons in schools using pioneering techniques with technology. He leads innovation and makes technology accessible to all educators. David embraces the idea of technology being used creatively to help all students learn. His blog has been recognised as one of the top three blogs in the UK for impact in education at the 2014 National UK Blog Awards, and influences classroom practice with technology around the world. David's work features in a wide variety of university research papers. He has also written a number of articles for the Guardian Teacher Network. David is a national speaker on creative use of technology and presents his work for the National Association of Headteachers.

**Christopher Dyer** is a primary school teacher in the North East of England, where he is currently curriculum leader for Computing. He has worked in a range of primary school settings developing a variety of ways to use digital technology to enhance children's learning. Christopher liaises with a number of local schools, advising them in the development of computing in their settings. He is the creator of the website **computinginprimaryschool.com**. This offers a variety of ideas, resources and support to implement the use of digital technology in the classroom.

**Clare Fenwick** is Senior Lecturer in Education for Primary Computing at Oxford Brookes University. Her teaching covers the effective use of technology and social media for learning as well as implementing the primary computing curriculum. She teaches both undergraduate and graduate students as well as delivering a range of continuous professional development for teachers and other school staff. Her sessions are delivered as online, blended or face to face. Her approach to teaching the primary computing curriculum focuses on the processes, problem solving and computational thinking rather than learning how to use specific devices and software, often taking an analogue approach. Her research area is the role of social media in learning.

**Sway Grantham** (@SwayGrantham) is a primary school teacher and Leader of Computing at Caroline Haslett Primary School. She has been ICT/Computing Leader since her NQT year and during this time has written a new curriculum and conducted research into the impact of 1:1 iPads in the primary classroom. Sway has been using technology all her life and has spent the last five years focusing this on education. She was invited as a 'lead learner' to attend the first ever Raspberry Picademy becoming a Raspberry Pi Certified Teacher and loves the opportunities these cheap computers offer. Recently having qualified as a Google Certified Teacher, Sway believes in offering children a range of ICT and Computing opportunities. Over the years, Sway has built up a successful blog (**www.swaygrantham.co.uk**), which is full of learning ideas and pedagogy for Computing, ICT and many other curriculum areas.

# Acknowledgements

Every effort has been made to trace the copyright holders and to obtain their permission for the use of copyright material. The publisher and author will gladly receive any information enabling them to rectify any error or omission in subsequent editions.

Helen Caldwell wishes to thank Ashley Williams for the images used in Figure 6.2. She also acknowledges the use of the image of Ferncumbe CofE Primary in Figure 6.3 shared under a CCby2.0 Licence at **http://commons.wikimedia.org/wiki/File:The_Ferncumbe_C_of_E_Primary_School_playground_-_geograph.org.uk_-_1757004.jpg** In addition, thank you to *Google Earth* for Figures 7.2 and 7.3, both Map image: *Google Earth* – Landsat, IBCAO and Data: SIO. NOAA. US Navy, NGA, GEBCO.

# Introduction

The use of technology in schools continues to evolve rapidly as new devices and tools become available, and the adoption of mobile devices such as iPads and tablets has been a particularly exciting development in recent years. The benefits offered by these technologies, such as their portability, connectivity, accessibility and range of media, present new challenges and opportunities for teaching and learning. As the take up of tablets gathers pace in our schools there is a need for advice on the best approaches and apps to help achieve successful learning outcomes. Teachers need to find meaningful ways to integrate the devices into their own practice and to evaluate which of the many thousands of educational apps might be appropriate for their pupils.

This book considers how iPads and tablets can be used to enhance teaching and learning in primary schools. It is especially relevant in the light of the computing curriculum, which puts a new emphasis on children as makers and creators of digital content. Across other curriculum subjects too, the introduction of mobile devices that can be quickly and reliably accessed has precipitated a shift in practice. For example, they have enabled teachers and children to spontaneously pursue lines of inquiry, to connect, collaborate and publish in many different ways, and to use their digital skills to enhance their exploration of the physical world outside the classroom.

With these opportunities in mind, we offer anecdotes from the classroom and examples of how tablets might be embedded within current pedagogy and practice as a natural learning tool. Each chapter combines a practical case study with discussion of related pedagogy, and recommends apps to support a personalised, inclusive and active approach to teaching and learning.

We begin in Chapter 1 by looking at how tablets make it easier to use a range of media to create shareable digital content such as movies, posters, animated characters, green screen effects or talking photos. Chapter 2 goes on to consider how these multimodal formats add value to eBooks and digital storytelling. Next, we consider how tablets can help make children's learning more visible by capturing learning activities through film, photos, screencasts and spoken explanations, making it easier to review learning and provide assessment opportunities. Chapter 4 explores ways in which the creative use of tablet apps can promote talk and collaboration with a particular focus on game-based learning. Our Early Years chapter explores the potential for making learning more personal and differentiated. Here we review apps for reinforcing numeracy and literacy skills in a motivating and accessible environment and consider their relevance to individual learning targets, thinking about how the customisation of content and pace can enhance inclusive practice. The following two chapters on 'Technology outdoors' and 'Children as researchers' outline the advantages of being able to use technology away from the traditional learning spaces of classrooms. We look at how tablets can add immediacy to researching topics and help children see themselves as information gatherers and creative producers. The final two chapters focus on computing, suggesting ways of using tablets to apply computational thinking skills to analyse and solve problems, and how children might make their own apps.

Drawing together these varied themes is the overarching concept of using tablets to build children's digital literacy. This encompasses skills such as choosing, evaluating and synthesising information with discrimination, learning how to build and create with technology, and collaborating and sharing with others safely. Our aim is to enthuse teachers and pupils as they develop these digital literacy skills through the use of tablets, and show how they can be used as a creative tool to engage with relevant challenges across all subject areas.

Helen Caldwell

January 2015

# Chapter 1

# Manipulating media

## Introduction

This chapter looks at how tablets make it easy to combine media to create shareable digital content such as movies, posters, animated characters, green screen effects or talking photos. An important aspect of digital literacy is the ability to combine media in meaningful ways, whether it is computer code, words, numbers, images, sound or video, and tablets can make it much easier to do this. Our 'Bridgecraft' case study explores the use of apps for creating purposeful digital artefacts. We will think about how the use of media can enable children to express their ideas and how it can enrich learning when it is used alongside other activities such as drama.

---

### Learning Objectives

At the end of this chapter you should be able to:

- identify a number of apps for working with film, animation, images, text and sound;
- understand how these apps can be used to combine media to create a range of digital artefacts;
- use some media apps to help children express their ideas and share them with an audience.

---

### Links to Teachers' Standards

The following Teachers' Standards are particularly relevant to this chapter:

TS1 Set goals that stretch and challenge pupils of all backgrounds, abilities and dispositions.
TS2 Demonstrate knowledge and understanding of how pupils learn and how this impacts on teaching.
Encourage pupils to take a responsible and conscientious attitude to their own work and study.
TS3 Have a secure knowledge of the relevant subject(s) and curriculum areas.
Foster and maintain pupils' interest in the subject, and address misunderstandings.
TS4 Promote a love of learning and children's intellectual curiosity.
Contribute to the design and provision of an engaging curriculum within the relevant subject area(s).

## Links to National Curriculum Programmes of Study

### Key Stage 1 and Key Stage 2

- Pupils become digitally literate – able to use, and express themselves and develop their ideas through information and communication technology – at a level suitable for the future workplace and as active participants in a digital world.
- All pupils are responsible, competent, confident and creative users of information and communication technology.
- Pupils should be taught to use technology purposefully to create, organise, store, manipulate and retrieve digital content.
- Pupils should be taught to select, use and combine a variety of software (including internet services), on a range of digital devices, to design and create a range of programs, systems and content that accomplish given goals, including collecting, analysing, evaluating and presenting data and information.

# Example from practice

*Bridgecraft: technology uniting physical and digital worlds*

**In the classroom**

## Context

Bridgewater Primary School in Northamptonshire held a curriculum enrichment week inspired by the world-building game *Minecraft*. Throughout the week, learning across the curriculum was based on the theme of helping to build an alternative *Bridgecraft* virtual world for some lost avatars. Each year group was responsible for a different element of the *Bridgecraft* world and children were challenged to produce a range of digital and physical artefacts. The ideas for using tablets outlined in the case study below were inspired by the project at Bridgewater Primary School, and are partly based on their work. We have emphasised the use of technology in order to suggest how tablets might be integrated into a similar whole-school project.

---

**Learning Objectives**

- to raise the profile of maths, science, art and technology through an integrated approach;
- to deepen children's thinking skills and give them opportunities to apply their knowledge to problem-solving situations;
- to help children see the relevance of maths and science in everyday life;
- to inspire the school community to work together and celebrate their learning with the local community.

---

## Outline

At the start of the week, an online avatar introduced the *Bridgecraft* project to the children during a whole-school assembly. She told them that her friends had lost their virtual world and asked if they could all work together to build a new world. In order to extend the games theme, the avatar explained that they would meet at the end of each day to celebrate their achievements and receive challenges that would unlock the next level. As each level was unlocked, the children received a clue or an object to help them complete the following day's challenge. In addition to the use of a games-based approach, there was an emphasis on integrating the arts with science and computing, and on using online collaboration tools to share ideas. Pairs of classes within the school were twinned – using the online networking tool *Edmodo*, so that they could share ideas – and a blog and *Twitter* feed invited participation from the wider world. At the end of the week, parents and members of the local community were invited to come into the school to explore the world of *Bridgecraft* through an exhibition of physical and digital artefacts.

A curriculum plan showing each year group's contributions to the project in computing, science and art is outlined below.

# Curriculum plan

**Table 1.1**   Curriculum plan

| | Computing | Science | Art |
|---|---|---|---|
| Year 1 Theme:<br>The Animals<br>(Clue: strange eggs)<br>Focus: Create animals for the world and design their habitats with help from Year 6. | Animated films.<br>Apps: *PuppetPals, Tellagami*<br>*iMovie* | Compare and contrast animals and their habitats<br>Carnivores, herbivores and omnivores | Explore colour, shapes and textures to make prints in the style of Paul Klee. |
| Year 2 Theme:<br>The Trees and Plants<br>(Clue: a giant seed)<br>Focus: Designing and making trees for the world. Work towards creating a large tree. | Working with images.<br>App: *Phoster*<br>Manipulating images of practical art.<br>Apps: *Snapseed, BeFunky, Haiku Deck, Skitch, PicCollage* | Plant life cycles<br>How plants grow | Abstract sculpture, batiq and textiles inspired by the work of Gustav Klimt. |
| Year 3 Theme:<br>The People<br>(Clue: a selection of hats)<br>Focus: Creating people for the world. | Creating movies.<br>Apps: *iMovie trailers, Morfo, Vintagio, GreenScreen by DoInk, ThingLink* | Human biology<br>Nutrition<br>Skeletons and muscles | Sewing and wire-modelling techniques in the style of Pablo Picasso. Creating book illustrations of characters. |
| Year 4 Theme:<br>The Sounds<br>(Clue: a piece of music)<br>Focus: What will our world sound like? Creating instruments, recording sounds and responding to art through music. | Composing music.<br>Apps: *GarageBand, VoiceThread, QuickVoice*<br>Creating abstract art in response to music.<br>App: *Fragment* | Sound and vibrations<br>Pitch and volume<br>Sound patterns and sources | Exploring art installations that use sound and abstract artists such as Wassily Kandinsky. |
| Year 5 Theme:<br>The Buildings<br>(Clue: a key)<br>Focus: The challenge of designing homes for the avatars. | Researching and designing houses.<br>Apps: *StreetView, Google Earth, Comic Life, PicCollage, Prezi, VideoScribe*<br>*Explain Everything* | Sustainability<br>Properties of materials<br>World cultures | Creating 3D sculptures in the style of Antoni Gaudi |
| Year 6 Theme:<br>The Homes and Habitats<br>(Clue: a strange nest)<br>Focus: Create homes and habitats for the animals. | Researching and designing animal homes and habitats.<br>Apps: *Haiku Deck, VoiceThread*<br>*VideoScribe*<br>*ThingLink* | Habitats<br>Animal classification systems<br>Food chains | Clay models based on the work of Joan Miro. |

We will describe how tablets and apps can be used to enhance learning across subjects in each year group.

### Exploring eggs: Year 1

Year 1 children focused on the animals of the virtual world and were inspired by the discovery of a nest of strange eggs. They made prints of imagined creatures in the artistic style of Paul Klee and photographed them with their tablets. They used descriptive language to develop their creatures' personas and shared their ideas as a mindmap, combining images and text using the *Popplet* app. The images were opened in the *PuppetPals* app, and children were able to 'cut out' the animals and move them around the screen using their fingers whilst recording their voices. The resulting animated puppet shows were exported and combined in *iMovie* to make a film introducing the *Bridgecraft* animals to show to parents at the end of the week, complete with added sound effects, music and credits. A talking avatar created in *Tellagami* was added to introduce the film.

### Inspired by seeds: Year 2

In Year 2, the impetus of a giant seed prompted work on designing and making trees and plants for the virtual world. Children walked around the local environment capturing images of plant life. These were digitally edited using a photo editor with a choice of filter effects using the apps *Snapseed* and *BeFunky*. Within these apps, children experimented with sliders and filters to alter the hue, saturation and contrast of their images in order to give the work an 'other-worldly' feel. They created names for their invented plants and trees. Some children went on to add descriptive text, choosing from a range of poster templates in the *Phoster* app; some used *PicCollage* to make an annotated collage; others used *Skitch* to add text and labels to their images. The results were combined in the slideshow app *Haiku Deck*, and embedded as a slideshow on the class blog.

### Inventing people: Year 3

Year 3's work was based around creating people for the virtual world. Beginning with the clue of a collection of hats, children produced group dramas based on characters who live, work or play together, thinking about their various roles and responsibilities. They filmed themselves talking in front of a *Minecraft* background, using the app *GreenScreen by DoInk*, to create an illusion of being within the game. They went on to design their characters within *Minecraft* and imported screenshots of these into the app *Morfo* to make animated talking heads. Working with *GreenScreen* techniques again, they made films of themselves interviewing their *Minecraft* characters. As an extension, some children created films in the style of silent movies using *Vintagio*, with added special effects using the app *Studio FX*. The resulting video clips were combined in *iMovie* to make a trailer in the style of an action movie introducing the people of *Bridgecraft*.

### Composing sounds: Year 4

Year 4 began their exploration of the sounds of the *Bridgecraft* world using a selection of real instruments, together with music apps such as *GarageBand, Glow Tunes, SoundPrism, LoopsequeKids, Musyc* and *Mix Tiki*. Their music-making was inspired by the abstract artwork of Klimt, Kandinsky and Miro, and tied in with science work on sound. After choosing a piece of abstract art, children thought about three emotional responses and used these to create a soundscape. They aimed to compose short responsive pieces, thinking about how the image inspired ideas about an imagined virtual world and capturing their digital and physical music-making using the app *QuickVoice*. Alongside this, they invented a method of writing down their pieces as a readable musical score. Some children went on to record sounds from their environment, analysing the waveforms, using the app *SoundOScope*, and combining them to compose loops using the *MadPad* app. To tie in with the art theme, they created their own accompanying abstract artworks using *Fragment*. Other children continued with the theme of combining sounds and art by exploring options to 'paint with sounds', using the apps *Singing Fingers* and *SoundBrush*. The finished works from the class were gathered together using *VoiceThread*, which allows for narration, text and sounds to be displayed alongside images and subsequently played through as a whole piece.

**Figure 1.1**   Recreating the *Bridgecraft* world in digital and physical media

### Designing buildings: Year 5

In Year 5, the focus was on the buildings of *Bridgecraft*. Children were given the clue of a key and the challenge of designing homes for the lost avatars. They used *Google Earth* and *Google Maps* to visit places on their iPads and took screenshots of buildings around the world. These were combined with research into the properties of materials and presented as explanatory screencasts, with annotations and narration. Children chose from the apps *Explain Everything*, *VideoScribe* and *Shadow Puppets Edu* to present their ideas.

### Creating habitats: Year 6

Year 6 children were given the stimulus of a strange nest and challenged to design animal homes and habitats using their knowledge of animal classification systems. They used *PicCollage* to collect images of the wildlife belonging to a particular habitat. These images were combined into a comic format, using the app *Strip Designer*. Hotspots added to these comic pages, using the app *ThingLink*, opened up excerpts of spoken narration, sound effects, explanatory text and close up images of the animals.

**Activity**

Many of these examples relied on combinations of apps. This is often referred to as 'app smashing'. Look at the list below and think about what is gained by putting two or three apps together. Create a plan to use one of these combinations in a curriculum area.

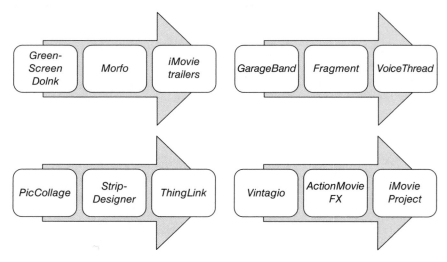

**Figure 1.2**   Example workflows using combinations of apps

Make a list of the more open-ended apps you currently use for manipulating media. Think of three ways in which these might be combined in pairs or trios to make a range of finished products. Reflect upon how this enhances children's learning.

# Discussion

We will look at ways of combining apps to facilitate media production. We will also consider the advantages of Bridgewater School's approach, in which tablets were used alongside practical science, art and design technology, and which brought in elements of games-based learning.

## Combining apps for an effective workflow

It is evident that tablets present new challenges to teachers, and many schools are finding that it is not enough just to add devices to classrooms without careful curriculum planning and evaluation. There are concerns about schools 'jumping on the iPad bandwagon' (Kobie, 2011), and that tablets might end up reinforcing drill and practice learning in much the same way as interactive whiteboards propagated didactic teaching (Alberta, 2012; Nocente and Belostotski, 2009). There is a need to balance freedom and choice for learners, and to provide a guiding framework (Melhuish and

Falloon, 2010). It is clear that careful thought needs to be given as to how best to use tablets to accelerate learning.

We have seen that one of the keys to the effective use of media with tablets is the fact that a small number of open-ended apps can be combined in various ways. To give an example: animated talking faces created in *Morfo*, *PuppetPals* animations and videos made with *GreenScreen by DoInk* on iPads automatically appear in *iMovie* as editable assets. Once in *iMovie*, these assets can be combined, edited and enhanced by sound effects – with impressive results. Another example is the way in which children's own artwork can be photographed and made into a comic strip using *Strip Designer*, and the comic then turned into an interactive image using *ThingLink*, so that characters talk when clicked and objects lead to new information.

Much can be achieved by drawing from a toolkit of apps that work together well. You might choose a video editor, a collage-maker, a screencasting tool, a sound recorder, a photo-editor, a comic format, a slideshow app and an animation tool. A goal can then be for children to become familiar with a handful of open-ended apps and to begin to make their own choices as to how to combine and use them, thereby developing more ownership over their learning.

## Choosing apps

An important aspect of our case study was the way in which the apps interacted with each other. By understanding how apps can work together, we can make the most of their particular affordances. Table 1.2 summarises the features of a number of media apps.

**Table 1.2** Media apps

| App | What it does |
| --- | --- |
| *PuppetPals* (iOS) | Screencasting |
| *Tellagami* (Android or iOS) | A talking avatar |
| *iMovie* (iOS) | Video editing and trailers |
| *Phoster* (iOS) | Poster templates |
| *Snapseed* (Android or iOS) | Photo editing |
| *Haiku Deck* (iOS) | Slideshow |
| *Skitch* (Android or iOS) | Image annotation |
| *PicCollage* (Android or iOS) | Collage |
| *GarageBand* (iOS) | Music composition |
| *VoiceThread* (iOS and web) | Respond to images through sound and text |
| *Fragment* (iOS) | Makes images abstract |
| *Morfo* (iOS and Windows) | Animate talking faces |

*(Continued)*

**Table 1.2**  (Continued)

| App | What it does |
|---|---|
| *GreenScreen by DoInk* (iOS) | Greenscreen filming |
| *VideoScribe* (iOS) | Present using hand-drawn animations |
| *Strip Designer* (iOS) | Comic strips |
| *ThingLink* (Android or iOS) | Interactive images |
| *Explain Everything* (Android or iOS) | Screencasting |
| *Shadow Puppets Edu* (iOS) | Images with narration |

A key idea is to evaluate what each app adds to the learning process. The SAMR (Substitution, Augmentation, Modification and Redefinition) model by Puentedura (2012) illustrates how judicious choices of apps might move learning through stages of substitution (doing the same thing in a different way), augmentation (adding something), modification (redesigning the task) through to redefinition (doing something you couldn't do before). It can be argued that at the redefinition stage, technology is helping to transform learning by focusing on higher order thinking skills. Evaluating what each app adds to the learning landscape in your own context is a useful starting point when you are making choices.

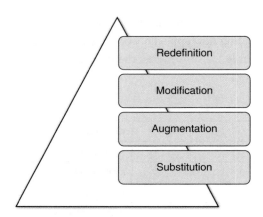

**Figure 1.3**  SAMR model showing the transformative potential of technology (Puentedura, 2012)

A study by Murray and Olcese (2011), looking at tablet use in schools, considered the idea of technology transforming learning by analysing apps in order to determine whether the iPad allows teachers and students *to do things in learning that could not otherwise be possible* (p43). They picked out a handful of apps which stood out for having the potential to extend learning opportunities through access to a virtual community, the effective use of media, and collaborative potential, but concluded that the majority of educational apps available at the time of writing were *out of synch with modern theories of learning* (p48), as they were narrowly focused on the consumption of content. This research highlights the importance of content creation and collaboration as areas that can extend learning by allowing for active knowledge construction within a social context.

Think about how a visual approach that mixes sound, images, animation, film, narration and text might offer multiple ways into a topic, supporting learners who find working with text challenging and inspiring all to be creative and ambitious. Offering children alternative forms of expression can encourage them to aim to produce a digital artefact that they are proud to share.

## Collaborative game-based learning

Another feature of our case study was the way in which elements of console games were used to 'hook' children into learning themes, just as games designers engage their players. Console game players learn to apply increasingly complex problem-solving techniques in order to achieve goals as they progress through a game. In a similar way, the Bridgewater teachers aimed to make their learning environment more effective by beginning with simple levels to help children feel successful and giving daily feedback on progress towards the shared goal of making the virtual world. Motivation was kept high, as teams of children encountered bonus tasks, came across new characters and objects, unlocked new levels and found clues as the week progressed.

## Social learning

The approaches to using media we have described are based on the notion that children are naturally social and learn through active knowledge-building rather than having an extrinsic curriculum imposed on them, concepts developed by many learning theorists, including Piaget (1979) and Papert (1994). In line with these ideas, recent researchers have noted the advantages of students working together in multimodal environments that integrate personal and shared learning spaces, promoting social learning and allowing teachers 'to weave more information from more sources into the classroom dialogue' (Fisher *et al.*, 2013, p166).

In our case study, the outcome was to create a shared vision of a new virtual world for a group of lost avatars. The tablets were used to communicate children's ideas of what this world might look like to an audience of peers and parents at the end of their enrichment week. The media manipulation apps allowed children to be digital creators in many different ways, from making a narrated slideshow presentation to creating a multimodal ebook.

Throughout the process of media making, then, children learned from and with each other, as they researched, created and shared content. The pursuit of an end goal is intrinsic to this process, as Turvey suggests: *Creativity has at its core a duality based upon the interplay between free exploration and more focused thinking as one moves towards an identified goal* (Turvey, 2006, p313).

For our children, online collaboration was a key to success. Pairs of classes from each year group were able to discuss progress towards their goals, using a private social platform provided by the app *Edmodo*. This gave them a chance to pose questions to the whole group without waiting for a turn, increasing pupil voice as they swapped strategies and posed questions for each other. Children's work in progress was also shared by mirroring their tablets onto the interactive whiteboard. These techniques streamlined the process of sharing ideas and gaining feedback, helping to keep learners focused and on track.

Children were encouraged to think about their audience from the beginning and to make decisions about the look and feel of their end products. Ideas were posted regularly onto the project blog, and each day began with a review of comments received from further afield. Having a focused theme and a known audience meant that children aimed to create work for others to see rather than for their teacher to mark, and it was noted that the immediate feedback from an authentic audience had a motivational effect, especially on the more reluctant writers.

## STEM to STEAM

The Bridgewater week also aimed to integrate science, computing and the arts, aligning with the STEM to STEAM movement's belief that an injection of the arts can add value to science, technology, engineering and maths, and that learning within all five subjects can be empowered by building on the natural overlaps between these subjects (Robelen, 2011; Burnard and Hennessey, 2006). Many researchers suggest that a cross-disciplinary approach uniting science and the arts fosters innovative thinking by drawing from the flexible perspectives and risk-taking associated with art-making. They suggest that such an approach has the potential to positively affect both our teaching and learning practices in schools and our economic competitiveness in the wider world (Platz, 2007; Freedman and Stuhr, 2004; Bequette and Bequette, 2012).

In our experience, the combination of creative arts, design technology and practical science paved the way for more personalised learning, and helped children to make connections across subjects as they worked towards a creative goal. Rather than always working in a digital environment, their physical artwork, drama role-plays or musical compositions were often used as the basis for a digital product. As an example of this process, ideas about the scientific process of plant growth were represented through animations based on original drawings.

The use of tablets meant that children could save photos of their own artwork and science investigations in the camera roll, alongside images from the internet and screenshots from apps. They could then draw from this personal bank of resources to make new media. Think about the benefits of children being able to research information in a form they find accessible, return to it in their own time and review it at their own pace. They can build up knowledge of a topic through a combination of listening, reading and viewing, and then remix media to convey their ideas in a final piece.

Your role as a teacher, when children are negotiating individual learning routes in this way, is to help them to see connections and areas of interest within a subject, and capture their thinking processes – using technology – so that you can help them make decisions about next steps. For example, you could use tablets to explore and structure ideas through mindmapping apps such as *Popplet*. Or, to take this idea further, you could make a physical 3D mindmap using circles and real objects on the floor to be shared as an image on a working wall, perhaps alongside drawings, photos, vocabulary and Quick Response (QR) codes pointing to relevant digital content. Be reassured that even the youngest children will be keen to explore alongside you and there is often no need to introduce new apps in a formal way; the idea of playful exploring or 'tinkering' is a key aspect of computational thinking. Finding out what apps and tablets can do is as intuitive to today's children as playing with modelling clay, and you need to bear in mind that not only is this technology part of their lives right now, it will be integral to their futures.

Allowing digital and physical ways of working, and for the arts and the sciences to complement each other as we have suggested, can deepen understanding of individual subjects. As Edelson puts it:

> *Authentic activities provide learners with the motivation to acquire new knowledge, a perspective for incorporating new knowledge into their existing knowledge, and an opportunity to apply their knowledge.*

(Edelson et al., 1999, p393)

And thinking about the wider learning context, linking creation and consumption – so that children produce digital products based on themes they have chosen to research – builds both media literacy and digital literacy. As independent creators, children learn to evaluate what each medium has to offer, and the process of making sharpens their critical awareness of the information they consume, making them more media-savvy. The end result we are aiming for is a generation of thoughtful and literate digital citizens.

---

### Activity

Look at the list of media apps in Table 1.2 and identify three ways in which they might be used to facilitate art meeting science in the primary curriculum. An example might be to make a *Haiku Deck* slideshow based on outdoor art, using natural objects illustrating the concepts of sun and shadows. Think about your role in making the most of the learning opportunities.

---

## Summary and Key Points

We have looked at how manipulating media, using tablets, can put children in control of pursuing their passions and sharing their creations. Our case study illustrated how elements of games-based learning might add challenge and structure to a classroom project, and placed a firm emphasis on children working together to achieve their goals. We also considered how physical art, music and drama might go hand in hand with the use of tablets, and how the creative subjects, science and technology can work in unison to amplify learning.

We have suggested that the media capabilities of tablets have the potential to support different modes of learning and that this versatility supports learners of all abilities. Tablets support anytime, anywhere learning and, when integrated with curriculum subjects in a purposeful way, they can extend learning beyond the classroom to informal learning contexts outside school. In addition, the process of engaging with media production can deepen children's awareness of the role of media in society and develop their critical understanding.

## Reflective Questions

To what extent does the idea of integrating the STEM subjects fit with your existing practice? Can you see added value in including the arts to move from STEM to STEAM?

What do you think are the main benefits of organising a whole school enrichment week? What are the advantages of using tablets to support whole school activities?

Our case study used tablets for pairs of classes to share their learning. Can you see ways in which this might enhance your own teaching and identify the first steps needed to implement this approach?

## Useful Links

### Bridgewater Primary STEAM week
https://showyou.com/v/y-jecVKxBrplA/bridgewater-primary-steam-week (accessed 20 December 2014).

### Tablets for learning: using Android apps in the classroom
https://slp.somerset.gov.uk/cypd/elim/somersetict/Computing_Curriculum_Primary/iPads%20and%20Tablets/Android%20apps%20for%20learning%20Dec%202013.pdf (accessed 20 December 2014).

A useful set of multimedia apps for Android devices.

### Northampton Inspire
http://mypad.northampton.ac.uk/inspire (accessed 20 December 2014).

A primary teacher network exploring the creative use of technology across the primary curriculum and looking at the theme of STEM to STEAM.

### Apps 4 Primary Schools
www.apps4primaryschools.co.uk (accessed 20 December 2014).

A site aimed at teachers looking for educational apps for preschool, Early Years, special educational needs and Key Stages 1 and 2. Filterable by age and subject and platform.

## Pinterest collection

**www.pinterest.com/helencaldwel** (accessed 20 December 2014).

A large collection of online resources and apps for teaching with digital technology, including iPads for maths, iPads for Key Stages 1 and 2, apps for EYFS/Key Stage 1, apps for literacy, apps for computing and STEM to STEAM.

# App List for the Chapter

*PicCollage, iBrainstorm, Popplet, VideoScribe, Strip Designer, Morfo, GreenScreen by DoInk, Haiku Deck, Snapguide, PixnTell, iMovie, Phoster, GarageBand, ThingLink, Snapseed, BeFunky, VoiceThread, PuppetPals, Tellagami, Skitch, QuickVoice, SoundPrism, SoundOScope, LoopsequeKids, Mix Tiki, Falling Stars, Glow Tunes, MadPad, SoundBrush, SingingFingers, VoiceThread, Vintagio, Studio FX, Explain Everything, Google Earth, Google Maps, Edmodo, Fragment, Musyc, Shadow Puppets Edu.*

# Further Reading

### The Visual in Learning and Creativity: A Review of the Literature

**www.creativitycultureeducation.org/wp-content/uploads/the-visual-in-learning-and-creativity-92. pdf** (accessed 20 December 2014).

A report for Creative Partnerships from Carey Jewitt at the Institute of Education, University of London.

### Games-based experiences for learning

**www.futurelab.org.uk/resources/games-based-experiences-learning** (accessed 20 December 2014).

A report from Futurelab at NFER discussing digital games and learning, and suggesting a set of design principles for planning games-based learning experiences.

### STEAM case studies

**http://stemtosteam.org/case-studies** (accessed 20 December 2014).

A site exploring the concept of integrating subjects through STEAM with case studies of these ideas in practice across education sectors.

### iPad Art Room

**www.ipadartroom.com** (accessed 20 December 2014).

Resources and ideas for using the SAMR Model to merge traditional art making with the use of tablets. There are two ebooks by Cathy Hunt to download, *Lessons, Apps and Ideas for the iPad in Visual Art* and *App-straction: Technology Enhanced Art Education*, an in-depth exploration of a creative, multimedia lesson. These books form part of the 'One Best Thing' collection of over 100 free ebooks written by Apple Distinguished Educators.

### Deploying and managing iOS devices in the classroom

**https://slp.somerset.gov.uk/cypd/elim/somersetict/appleblog/eLIM%20Genius%20Bar%20 Documents/Deploying%20and%20Managing%20iOS%20Devices.pdf** (accessed 20 December 2014).

A practical guide to options for charging and syncing a set of iPads and how to buy and license apps for schools from eLIM Somerset.

# References

Alberta (2012) iPads: What are we learning? Available from: **http://education.alberta.ca/admin/technology/research.aspx** (accessed 18 January 2014).

Bequette, JW and Bequette, MB (2012) A place for art and design education in the STEM conversation. *Art Education*, 65(2), 40–7.

Burnard, P and Hennessy, S (eds) (2006) *Reflective Practices in Arts Education* (Vol. 5). Netherlands: Springer.

Edelson, DC, Gordin, DN and Pea, RD (1999) Addressing the challenges of inquiry-based learning through technology and curriculum design. *Journal of the Learning Sciences*, 8(3/4), 391–450. Available from: http://www.geode.northwestern.edu/userdownloads/pdf/JLSEdelsonetal.pdf (accessed 20 December 2014).

Fisher, B, Lucas, T and Galstyan, A (2013) The role of iPads in constructing collaborative learning spaces. *Technology, Knowledge and Learning*, 18(3), 165–78.

Freedman, K and Stuhr, P (2004) Curriculum change for the 21st century: Visual culture in art education. *Handbook of Research and Policy in Art Education*, 815–28.

Gardner, H (1983) *Frames of Mind*. New York: Basic Books Inc.

Johnson, L, Adams, S, Cummins, M, Estrada, V, Freeman, A and Ludgate, H (2013) The NMC Horizon Report: 2013 Higher Education Edition.

Keengwe, J and Bhargava, M (2013) Mobile learning and integration of mobile technologies in education. *Education and Information Technologies*, 1–10.

Kobie, Nicole (2011) The school that swapped its laptops for iPads … and wants to switch back. 11 September 2011. Available from: **http://www.pcpro.co.uk/blogs/2012/09/11/the-school-that-swapped-its-laptops-for-ipads-and-wants-to-switch-back** (accessed 18 January 2014).

Melhuish, K and Falloon, G (2010) Looking to the future: M-learning with the iPad. *Computers in New Zealand Schools*, 22(3), 1–16.

Murray, OT and Olcese, NR (2011) Teaching and learning with iPads, ready or not? *TechTrends*, 55(6), 42–8.

Nocente, N and Belostotski, G (2009) Elementary and junior high school use of clickers. *In World Conference on E-Learning in Corporate, Government, Healthcare, and Higher Education*, 2009( 1), 999–1008.

Papert, S (1994) *The Children's Machine: Rethinking School in the Age of the Computer*. New York: Harvester Wheatsheaf.

Piaget, J (1979) *Six Psychological Studies*. Brighton: Harvester Press.

Platz, J (2007) How do you turn STEM into STEAM? Add the Arts! Available from: **http://www.ikzadvisors.com/wp-content/uploads/2009/09/STEM-+-ARTS-STEAM.pdf** (accessed 20 December 2014).

Puentedura, R (2010) *SAMR and TPCK: Intro to Advanced Practice*. Available from: **http://goo.gl/78UJn** (accessed 18 January 2014).

Robelen, EW (2011) STEAM: Experts make case for adding arts to STEM. *Education Week*, 31(13), 8.

Turvey, K (2006) Towards deeper learning through creativity within online learning communities in primary education. *Computers and Education*, 46, 309–21.

# Chapter 2

# Digital storytelling

## Introduction

In this chapter we will consider how multimodal formats add value to ebooks and digital storytelling, and explore the potential for using tablets to make ebooks personalised and differentiated. We will also demonstrate how to create a range of ebooks featuring both narrative and non-narrative texts. A review of apps to create ebooks which can reinforce numeracy, literacy and computing skills in an interactive digital content, and a consideration of their relevance to individual children's learning targets and needs, will also be highlighted. A further area of focus will be the potential for customising ebooks by including photos, videos, activities, text or sound to provide content targeted at children's needs and interests. We will suggest strategies to support individual learning goals and discuss how ebooks can be shared in order to promote peer assessment and collaboration.

To be literate in today's digital world, children need to familiarise themselves with a range of technologies and software. Electronic books can provide primary aged children with a range of content experiences and can have a number of benefits. Although we would not suggest that they replace paper books, ebooks can provide motivating and interactive reading experiences. In addition, making ebooks can enable children to draw upon their own experiences, personalising their learning and making it real and purposeful. Our three ebook case studies show how a Year 3 class explored ways of working with ebooks in English, maths and history. In history, the whole class worked collaboratively to create an ebook based on the topic of Ancient Egypt (case study 1); in maths, the teacher created an ebook as a resource to support mathematical understanding (case study 2); and in English, children created individual ebook stories, incorporating a range of digital features (case study 3).

---

### Learning Outcomes

At the end of this chapter you should be able to:

- identify a number of apps that can be combined to create ebooks;
- understand how to make ebooks and their value in the primary setting;

*(Continued)*

---

*(Continued)*

- identify a number of ways in which ebooks can help support children's learning;
- apply some of these techniques to help children express their own ideas and share them with an audience.

## Links to Teachers' Standards

The following Teachers' Standards are particularly relevant to this chapter:

TS1 Set goals that stretch and challenge pupils of all backgrounds, abilities and dispositions.

TS2 Demonstrate knowledge and understanding of how pupils learn and how this impacts on teaching.

Encourage pupils to take a responsible and conscientious attitude to their own work and study.

TS3 Have a secure knowledge of the relevant subject(s) and curriculum areas.

Foster and maintain pupils' interest in the subject, and address misunderstandings.

TS4 Contribute to the design and provision of an engaging curriculum within the relevant subject area(s).

TS5 Know when and how to differentiate appropriately, using approaches which enable pupils to be taught effectively.

TS6 Give pupils regular feedback, both orally and through accurate marking, and encourage them to respond to the feedback.

## Links to National Curriculum Programmes of Study

### Key Stage 1 and Key Stage 2

- Pupils become digitally literate – able to use, and express themselves and develop their ideas through information and communication technology – at a level suitable for the future workplace and as active participants in a digital world.
- Pupils use technology purposefully to create, organise, store, manipulate and retrieve digital content.
- Pupils select, use and combine a variety of software (including internet services) on a range of digital devices to design and create a range of programs, systems and content that accomplish given goals, including collecting, analysing, evaluating and presenting data and information.

# Example from practice

## Case study 1

*Creating an information text ebook about Ancient Egypt: Year 1*

**In the classroom**

## Context

Over the course of a term, a Year 3 class at Wheatley Hill Primary School, County Durham worked together to create an ebook about Ancient Egypt for the school's iBook library, which would become available for the whole school to use as a resource. Pairs of children chose an area of interest and were jointly responsible for making a page in the ebook. The children added a range of widgets, such as quiz questions and hotspots, to make their pages interactive.

> **Learning Objectives**
>
> - to create an ebook about Ancient Egypt;
> - to record and share our learning with the wider school community;
> - to write a piece of information text;
> - to add a range of multimedia content.

## Outline

The children completed a series of six sessions to create the ebook. These are outlined below.

**Table 2.1** Planning overview

| Session | Learning Objective | Activity | Resources |
|---|---|---|---|
| 1 | To decide upon an area of interest. | Pupils are introduced to the task of creating an ebook about Ancient Egypt. They add the period to the class timeline. Pupils decide, in pairs, upon a specific area of interest. There is a whole class discussion on the layout of the ebook (title, content and pages). | Timeline |
| 2 + 3 | To use primary and secondary sources to collect information. | The teacher explains the need to find as much information as possible about their chosen area of interest. Pupils use a range of both primary and secondary resources to collect information. They record their findings using digital technology. | Textbooks<br>iPads<br>Internet<br>Artefacts |
| 4 | To plan a page for the ebook | The teacher shares an example page in *iBook Author*. Pupils discuss its page layout. They then use the *Explain Everything* app to design their page, including heading, text and images. | iPads<br>*Explain Everything* app |

*(Continued)*

**Table 2.1** (Continued)

| Session | Learning Objective | Activity | Resources |
|---------|-------------------|----------|-----------|
| 5 | To create a page for the ebook. | The teacher demonstrates using tools in *iBook Author*. Pupils use *iBook Author* to create their page. They put together all their findings into one page. | MacBook *iBook Author* Pupils' research |
| 5 | To add multimedia content to the page. | The teacher explains to pupils how they can add interactive widgets to page in *iBook Author* to create multimedia content. Pupils in pairs add a widget to their page. | MacBook *iBook Author* |
| 6 | To present your work. | The teacher and the children add ebook to the school's online library (iBooks). The ebook is displayed on the interactive whiteboard via air server. Pupils present their page to the rest of the class and await feedback. | MacBook |

The children completed a series of sessions (see Table 2.1) to create an ebook. They were able to make clear progress by using a range of apps and features on an iPad, as well as the MacBook, to reach their learning outcomes. At the start, the whole class decided upon the page they would be completing, then pairs of children decided upon an area of interest. This gave each child a clear understanding of the ebook layout.

Thought was given to how to support a range of abilities when engaging in internet research. My lower ability pupils were given a limited number of websites to use as sources, whereas the higher ability children had more freedom to explore for themselves. Similarly, some children were provided with sets of images, writing prompts and relevant vocabulary. For others the task was much more open-ended.

When the children collected information for themselves, they were able to use the camera app to take photographs of primary resources – as well as screen shots from relevant textbooks – to store digitally and add to their page at a later date. They used the presentation app *Keynote* to document their research, making it easy to access and review their work. Children of all abilities could access this task, as some could simply take photographs while others could be responsible for typing, and the use of images provided support for their writing. Once children had completed their research, they were able to use the *Explain Everything* app to plan the design of their page, making each page unique.

An additional advantage of using the iPad for online research was the 'Speak Selection' feature, which enabled children to listen to highlighted text read aloud. This not only provided support for reading but facilitated the editing of writing, as children could listen for errors or omissions and identify ways in which they could improve their word choices.

Some children used the *Morfo* app to create talking characters. Using a Creative Commons licensed image of an Egyptian face sourced from an Advanced Search on *Google* or *Flickr*, they were able to create an animation which lip-synced with their own recorded speech. This meant that they could adopt the role of an Egyptian and express their thoughts and feelings in role. Once these were created, the children e-mailed or saved them to *Dropbox* to add to their page in a video format.

As soon as the children had collected their information and planned their pages, they were ready to create the ebook. I set up *iBook Author* on the MacBooks in advance for them to create their page by specifying the book cover, the number of pages and the contents page. Each pair was allocated a blank page and they were able to access their previously e-mailed work as a starting point.

There were many opportunities for children to demonstrate their computing skills throughout the unit, but the addition of a range of widgets to the book pages was a useful source of differentiation. The widgets are a special feature in *iBook Author* on a Mac computer, allowing the user to add multimedia content such as a gallery, types of media, quiz questions, interactive images, a scrolling sidebar, a 3D image or a pop-over. For example, a lower ability pair might add a simple 3D image to their page, which moves when touched to make a 3D effect. The high ability pairs investigated more complex widgets, such as multiple choice questions which responded with a green tick when the correct response was chosen.

In the final session the children presented their work to the whole class using *Air Server* to mirror the iPads to the interactive whiteboard. They discussed their end products and talked about areas which could be further developed and improved. This allowed me to access their final pieces of work and evaluate the way in which the pupils related to the development of the work. It also provided a rich source of peer feedback.

This eBook is available to watch at: **www.youtube.com/watch?v=5O9WBKYXn1Y** (accessed 20 December 2014).

## Case study 2

*Maths revision ebook: Year 3*

## Context

A Year 3 class at Wheatley Hill Primary School used a mathematical ebook created by their teacher as a lesson starter each week for a term. The theme of the ebook was multiplication. The aim was to enable children to complete a series of tasks independently and share them electronically with the teacher. Pupils accessed the ebook in PDF form, using an app called *Showbie*.

> ### Learning Objectives
>
> - to develop pupils' understanding of multiplication;
> - to share work and feedback electronically over the Internet;
> - to promote self-directed learning and give children more control over the pace of their learning.

My first tasks were to create the ebook, using the *Book Creator* app, and to create logins for children to access the app *Showbie*, which was key to the success of this project. My idea was to make a simple ebook all about times tables; this would include a front cover, and then a page for each times table. On each page I added some example number sentences based on the table, as well as an image illustrating the number facts. In addition, I was able to insert message prompts to give guidance to children who found the task difficult.

Next, the app *Showbie* was added to my class set of iPads. I created a *Showbie* teacher's account as well as individual accounts for the class. *Showbie* allows teachers to assign, collect and review student work, and it connects to a range of iPad apps. This allows greater connectivity and makes it easier to save and review work.

When I logged into my teacher's account, I simply added a new class named Year 3 and received a five-digit code, which was added to each child's account to match their *Showbie* account with the teacher's. I was then ready to go.

I opened my ebook and exported it as a PDF to my *Showbie* account and into a new file called 'Year 3'. Once a week, in my maths lesson starters, children logged on to Showbie using their unique username and password, selected the ebook and then scrolled to the multiplication table they were working on. They were able to use *Showbie* to annotate the book page with their answers. Pupils enjoyed completing the tasks and their motivation to practise times tables increased.

In the example above, children demonstrated their understanding of multiplication tables using the annotation tools in Showbie. If they found it difficult to write on the screen, there was an option to zoom into the image, and if they made a mistake they were able to use the rubber icon or click the undo button. The prompt on the page provided a reminder of strategies, and if they needed further help they could click on the note icon and tell me if they found the question too hard or even too easy. Then, once they had finished, they would click 'done' and the ebook would automatically save to their work space in PDF format.

I was able to observe the children's progress from my *Showbie* teacher's account. A paper clip icon next to their names indicated that they had completed their page and I could point the early finishers towards extension tasks. I was able to mark each child's work online and give constructive feedback by clicking on their name and opening their work. When I assess a piece of work I have the same annotation tools as the children, but mine appear in red. I give ticks and written feedback in note form, just as I would in their exercise books. Once I have marked their work a red circle appears, indicating to the children that they can access their feedback. They can then amend any mistakes and print out selected work to stick in their books for evidence.

After a few weeks of trialling the multiplication tables book, I began to create differentiated ebooks so that children could work on tasks that matched their ability. We also experimented with opening the ebooks in *Book Creator*, so that I could support their learning further by adding voice prompts and spoken feedback.

## Case study 3

*Create your own narrative ebook: Year 3*

## Context

For our third exploration of ebooks, my Year 3 class planned and wrote fairytale stories using *The Literacy Shed's Clocktower* film as a stimulus. Pupils used the *Book Creator* app to create ebooks, which were later shared with the rest of the school via the iBooks online library.

---

### Learning Objectives

- to write a piece of narrative text;
- to create an ebook;
- to enhance writing skills through the production of eBooks;
- to share digital work on an online platform.

---

First, the children watched the *Clocktower* clip available on *The Literacy Shed*. See **www.literacyshed.com/the-fairy-tale-shed.html** (accessed 20 December 2014). Then they planned their own stories about how the beautiful little girl ended up in the clocktower.

This ebook is available to watch at: **www.youtube.com/watch?v=qg8vZC3xCEw_** and the animation technique can be seen here: **www.youtube.com/watch? v=NBY3sIsggtY**

Children were able to use features in *Book Creator*, such as adding photos, drawings, text, narration, sound effects and video to create a media-rich ebook (see Figure 2.1). From the start, the children were engaged and enthused. I noted that individual children had many more choices than they usually do with pen and paper. They could amend the font and size of text or use the Speak Selection tool to check for errors. They could rewrite and edit as much as they wished, and at a pace that suited them. The use of words, images, video and narration meant that they could choose any combination of these methods to tell their story and still produce a professional looking book. Many chose to add a sound button to record themselves reading the story. This supported both the writers in capturing their ideas and, later, the readers, making the books accessible to a wider age group.

There was a good deal of potential in using digital art tools to enhance the storytelling. For example, children created a clocktower animation using a mosaic effect based on their own physical artwork, together with the stop frame animation app *iMotion* to turn hundreds of photographs into a short animation that could be inserted into the ebook as a video.

Once the ebooks were created we explored a number of publishing options, such as making a printed copy, adding it to our school iBook library as an ebook for all year groups to read and even publishing it on *YouTube* as a video. I used an app called *PS Mobile* to print ebooks in physical form for evidence. I also used the *Showbie* app to enable children to give feedback to their peers and suggest improvements. The children's ebooks were uploaded onto an area in *Showbie* that allowed them to save a copy onto their own digital device at home.

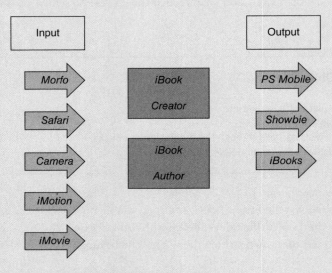

**Figure 2.1**  A flow chart of apps for making ebooks

Overall, our ebooks case studies have featured a range of apps which the children used independently to add rich layers of media to their ebooks. The diagram above summarises how these apps can be combined to help create an ebook. This is by no means an exhaustive list: children can choose from a wide range of apps to add interest through multimedia content. Adding photographs of their original artwork or animations made with their own model-making can also have a very powerful impact.

# Discussion

## Ebooks in the primary classroom

We have suggested that children need to be comfortable with a range of devices and tools if they are to be digitally literate by today's standards. Carlson (2004) proposes that technology is accelerating change at an even more rapid pace than we expected and, as Clark and Luckin (2013) and Traxler (2010) suggest, mobile devices such as iPads and tablets are fast becoming an essential classroom tool. Teachers need to share ways in which they enhance learning so that they are:

> *recognising the potential of new and emerging technologies and enabling their*
> *meaningful integration in support of teaching and learning.*
>
> (Alberta Education, 2010, p5)

One area highlighted throughout this chapter is the making and sharing of ebooks, also known as multi-touch textbooks. Using ebooks can enable teachers to promote independent learning, to differentiate learning more easily to accommodate a variety of abilities and to easily share resources. Our approach has been to use the ebook format to develop children's ideas and support them as they work at their own pace and level. We noted that children were able to develop a better understanding of a topic, as well as gain key English skills, by using a range of digital devices and techniques to create and merge multimedia content for their ebooks. We would agree with Clark and Luckin (2013) that a key benefit of mobile devices is the way in which they can work in combination with other technologies to support collaborative and personalised learning experiences. We will explore this idea further.

## Using ebooks for personalised learning

One advantage of the ebook format is the potential to personalise children's learning. We have shown that it can enable children to study any area of a given topic that interests them. For example, they can combine images from the internet, their own photographs, media created in other apps and physical artwork that they have created themselves. They can even add their own voice-overs, and they have a good deal of control over the pace of their work and the combination of media in the finished product. We think that being able to choose from a number of options increases children's motivation and engagement. As Loveless and Dore (2002) suggest, such choices promote independent learning as children can make informed judgements about what pieces of digital content they want to add to their ebook. They also have a greater sense of ownership over their work, which can improve productivity. This was clearly shown in case study 1, as the ebook created about Ancient Egypt was of a high standard and the children put a good deal of time and effort into it. The knowledge that the finished artefact was going to be published and shared with an audience provided additional impetus. Once the ebooks were available in the school's iBooks library, peers of all abilities across the primary age range could read them. Readers as young as five and six were accessing the ebook by scrolling through the pages, browsing the photo galleries and 3D images and listening to the text read aloud.

## Differentiation and accessibility

When our children created their ebooks they not only had the teacher to support them, but a range of options to help them along the way. We have summarised some of these in the table below.

**Table 2.2**  Tablet accessibility options supporting ebook writing

| Option | What it does | Where to find it |
|---|---|---|
| *Speak Selection* | Allows any selected text to be read aloud. | Once enabled in the iPad settings it becomes an option when selecting text. |
| *Text Size* | Adjusts text to your preferred reading size. | In the iPad general settings. |
| *Voice messages* | Enables the teacher to give hints, prompts or feedback. | An option within the *Showbie* app. |
| *Siri for Voice Recognition* | Turns your speech into text. | An iPad settings option. |
| *Guided Access* | Locks children into an app and restricts the use of a password. | In the iPad accessibility options. |
| *Invert colours* | Inverts the colours for more contrast, which some children prefer. | In the iPad accessibility options. |
| *Stylus* | An alternative to using a finger, useful for more precision when drawing or writing. | A bought extra. |

In addition to this, I was able to scaffold the ebook-making process by assigning specific tasks and differentiated support to groups and individuals. In case study 3, some children benefited from a simple layout of the story to help plan their work. Others were helped by having the option to add different levels of multimedia content. We would agree with Williams and Easingwood (2006) that technology should not replace the practical, hands-on element of teaching but it can give children alternative ways of researching a topic and sharing what they know. The use of sound or symbol support for reading and writing, for example, can help children with writing challenges to access learning and communicate independently. The Guided Access option can be used to restrict choices during an activity and help children with lower concentration spans stay focused. In this way, the technology can increase access and control over curriculum content for some children.

One outcome highlighted by our case studies was the positive impact of using images to inspire writing. Some of our children struggled with ideas or thoughts when handwriting, but the iPads gave them a visual focus that resulted in a high level of engagement and, in our opinion, a deeper understanding of the subject.

There is also the potential to explore other apps for storytelling. We plan to extend our work by exploring the following options:

- retelling traditional tales by making a narrated screencast in *PuppetPals*;

- creating a comic strip version using *Strip Designer*;

- making a talking book with *Shadow Puppets Edu*;

- animating a story with *iCanAnimate*;

- capturing drama in front of a greenscreen and adding backgrounds usng *GreenScreen by DoInk*;

- planning stories using *Popplet*.

## Collaboration

Another key outcome was the facility for pairs and groups to collaborate using the iPads and for me, as the teacher, to give responsive and timely feedback. The *Showbie* app had several advantages as a feedback tool. It could be accessed from any device, as children saved their work onto their personal online area. We could all access this online space, making marking easier and also facilitating peer feedback, as children could view each other's work online. I was able to add annotations, voice notes or even text notes directly onto the students' work and share these with them straight away.

---

**Activity**

Use the planning overview table in Figure 2.1 to plan your own ebook based on a historical theme. Aim to adapt it to your chosen topic.

---

**Summary and Key Points**

This chapter has explored ways in which tablets can help create ebooks and support children's learning across the curriculum. It has highlighted how teachers can incorporate the use of tablets into their everyday teaching, to enable children to create digital stories with visual media, interactivity and sound. These might include varying amounts of media content depending on levels of ability, but children can still end up with a satisfying end product. We have thought about some ways in which the use of tablets can help to meet a range of learning needs, as well as providing highly individual ways for children to demonstrate their ideas and understanding.

Our twenty-first-century learners have an increasing range of digital devices at their fingertips, and we have an exciting role as educators to use this to engage and develop children's learning as well as preparing them for the digital world they will face in later life.

## Useful Links

### A blog and YouTube examples from the project described in this chapter

www.computinginprimaryschools.com/ibooks and www.youtube.com/channel/UCvJxYQ5Hg8 YS6j5EzWMWn8g (accessed 20 December 2014).

### Ideas for creating multi-touch books

www.bookwidgets.com (accessed 20 December 2014).

### Evaluating the evidence

www.tabletsforschools.org.uk (accessed 20 December 2014).

A site collating research experience from teachers, industry leaders and academics on how tablets can impact learning and attainment.

### Fifty ways to tell a story

http://50ways.wikispaces.com (accessed 20 December 2014).

## App List for the Chapter

*Camera, Morfo, Keynote, Explain Everything, Dropbox, Book Creator, Showbie, PuppetPals, Strip Designer, Shadow Puppets Edu, ICanAnimate, Popplet, GreenScreen by DoInk, iMotion, Safari, iMovie, PS Mobile, iBooks.*

## Further Reading

### iPads in the Classroom

www.computinginprimaryschools.com/ipads-in-the-classroom (accessed 20 December 2014).

Ideas on how to use iPads in the primary classroom as well as downloadable ebook resources.

## References

Alberta Education (2010) *Emerge one-to-one laptop learning initiative: Final report. Edmonton.* Available from: www.education.alberta.ca/admin/technology/emerge- one-to-one.aspx (accessed 25 August 2014).

Carlson, G (2004) *Digital Media in the Classroom.* Gilroy, CA: CMP Books.

Clark, W and Luckin, R (2013) *What research says: iPads in the Classroom.* London: Knowledge Lab. Available from: https://www.lkldev.ioe.ac.uk/lklinnovation/wp-content/uploads/2013/01/2013-iPads-in-the-Classroom-v2.pdf (accessed 25 August 2014).

Loveless, A and Dore, B (2002) *ICT in the Primary School.* Buckingham: Open University Press.

Traxler, J (2010) Will student devices deliver innovation, inclusion, and transformation? *Journal of the Research Center for Educational Technology,* 6(1), 3–15.

Williams, J and Easingwood, N (2006) *Primary ICT and the Foundation Subjects.* London: Continuum International publishing group.

# Chapter 3

# Visible learning

## Introduction

This chapter looks at how tablets can help make children's learning more visible by capturing learning activities through film, photos, screencasts and spoken explanations, and by creating contexts for talk, making it easier to review learning and to provide assessment opportunities. Tablets have given us a whole new range of possibilities when it comes to children demonstrating their progress and understanding of a topic. No longer are they restrained by the challenge of putting pen to paper; instead, they can type, record their voice, use voice to text or simply make a screencast video. We will use the term 'visible learning' to describe the idea of using tablets to capture learning as it happens in the classroom. Visible learning coexists alongside everyday classroom activities to ensure that the teacher gets a greater insight into the learning that is happening within the classroom.

The following case study from Caroline Haslett School, Milton Keynes, models simple and practical ways to capture learning as, and when, it happens. It focuses on the different stages within the learning cycle at which children's learning can be recorded, and considers the depth necessary to inform teaching and learning throughout a topic of work. A range of apps is explored, along with open-ended examples of how to use them and a rationale explaining the pedagogical choices made.

We will go on to discuss how using tablets to allow insight into children's learning can enhance the learning experience by facilitating independent learning skills such as self-efficacy, learning about learning and self-assessment. We will also explore the impact for children when their learning is frequently shared with others, including their peers and their teacher, as well as further assessment opportunities that would not be possible without tablets. Capturing and sharing children's learning using tablets opens a wealth of possibilities for Assessment for Learning strategies (AfL), personalised learning and self-regulated learning.

## Learning Objectives

At the end of this chapter you should be able to:

- identify a number of apps for capturing learning through film, photos, screencasts and spoken explanations;
- understand how these apps can be used as assessment opportunities to inform Assessment for Learning (AfL);
- understand how these apps can coexist with traditional teaching methods, thus offering a wider range of learning experiences;
- apply some of these ideas to help children capture and share their learning.

## Links to Teachers' Standards

The following Teachers' Standards are particularly relevant to this chapter:

TS1 Establish a safe and stimulating environment for pupils.
Set goals that stretch and challenge pupils of all backgrounds, abilities and dispositions.
TS2 Demonstrate knowledge and understanding of how pupils learn and how this impacts on teaching.
Encourage pupils to take a responsible and conscientious attitude to their own work and study.
TS3 Have a secure knowledge of the relevant subject(s) and curriculum areas.
Foster and maintain pupils' interest in the subject, and address misunderstandings.
TS4 Promote a love of learning and children's intellectual curiosity.
Contribute to the design and provision of an engaging curriculum within the relevant subject area(s).
TS5 Have a clear understanding of the needs of all pupils, including: those with special educational needs; those of high ability; those with English as an additional language; those with disabilities; and to be able to use and evaluate distinctive teaching approaches to engage and support them.
Demonstrate a critical understanding of developments in the subject and curriculum areas, and promote the value of scholarship.

## Links to National Curriculum Programmes of Study

### Key Stage 1 and Key Stage 2

- pupils become digitally literate – able to use, and express themselves and develop their ideas through information and communication technology – at a level suitable for the future workplace and as active participants in a digital world;
- pupils are responsible, competent, confident and creative users of information and communication technology;
- pupils use technology purposefully to create, organise, store, manipulate and retrieve digital content;
- pupils select, use and combine a variety of software (including internet services) on a range of digital devices to design and create a range of programs, systems and content that accomplish given goals, including collecting, analysing, evaluating and presenting data and information.

# Example from practice

*A one-year trial of 1:1 iPads in a Year 5 class*

In the
classroom

## Context

During the academic year 2013–14, 32 children in Year 5 at Caroline Haslett Primary School participated in a 1:1 trial using iPads as a learning tool. One of the outcomes I noted was the way in which the iPads provided opportunities for children to share their work and discuss their learning. In this section, I will discuss a number of apps that helped to make learning more 'visible' to both the children within my class, and to me as their teacher.

> ### Learning Objectives
>
> - to encourage children to verbalise their thought processes;
> - to share the learning process so that it can be discussed and built upon;
> - to allow children to present their learning in a range of different ways;
> - to engage children in their own learning journey and empower them to share it with others.

## Outline

At Caroline Haslett Primary School, I began to use a variety of apps and media to capture, or make visible, the learning that was happening in my classroom. As such, Visible Learning' is a strategy I used alongside other learning activities across the curriculum.

## Visible learning cycle

Over the course of a lesson, or a series of lessons, I found that there were several stages at which I could use apps to make the learning process more explicit. This allowed me to delve deeper into the children's understanding and make them more aware of the progress they were making. The stages at which I capture learning form a cycle that can be roughly broken down into:

- Pre-/Post-assessment: this involves checking what children already know at the beginning of a lesson and then repeating the process at the end of the lesson or unit to check that they have learned what I was trying to teach them.

- Capturing learning live: this is a visual learning technique unique to tablets, as you can capture the process rather than just the outcome, allowing you to question how children arrive at their answers.

- Pit stops or mini plenaries: checking in with children throughout a lesson and ensuring that they are working in the right direction.

- Reflecting on learning: alongside capturing learning, tablets can make it quick and easy for children to explain exactly *why* they made choices and to demonstrate their understanding of a topic.

- Ongoing learning maps: these are a simple but effective way of making a visual representation of children's progress.

These stages are illustrated in Figure 3.1 below to demonstrate the learning journey over the course of a classroom topic. By following one of these routes from beginning to end, you will assemble a catalogue of visual learning evidence allowing you to adapt and meet the specific learning needs of the students in your class.

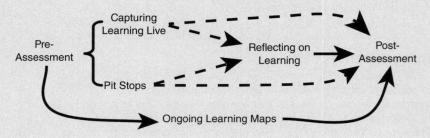

**Figure 3.1**   The visible learning cycle making children aware of their progress

We will look at how this cycle can be implemented over some example literacy, maths and design and technology lessons to see how it can enhance learning across the curriculum.

## Literacy lesson

### Pre-assessment

Using the app *Answer Garden*, I gave my class two minutes to 'List as many prepositions as you can.' Their answers instantly appeared on my interactive whiteboard (IWB) via the *Answer Garden* website. Once the children had submitted their answers, I immediately had a clear picture of which children had good ideas, and which found the task more challenging. Usually, I would focus my questioning on the one or two who were unsure, so as to ascertain whether this was due to a lack of understanding. However, in this case, there were five or six children who seemed to lack confidence. With this in mind, I launched a pre-prepared multiple-choice quiz using the app *Socrative* to ask them to explain what a preposition was and encourage them to pick out an example preposition from a selection of words.

Having used these apps to complete a pre-assessment for my class's existing knowledge of prepositions, I began my main literacy lesson. The lesson focus was on using prepositions in descriptive writing and the context was describing the interior of the Tardis from the *Dr Who* TV series. *Answer Garden* now worked for us as a word bank of examples – supporting those less confident at using prepositions, as well as forming a reminder of our language focus. The children wrote their descriptions into their literacy books and I continued my usual routine of reminding children to work on their literacy targets and checking in with those who had previously completed the *Socrative* quiz.

### Pit stop and reflection on learning

Around halfway through the lesson, I wanted to check that everyone had remembered to include the prepositions we talked about at the beginning. I asked the children to take a photo of the work they had written so far and use the app *Skitch* to annotate their images, highlighting examples of prepositions. Next, they used a website called *Padlet*, a virtual wall for posting and sharing, to display the annotated image of their written work. We were able to look at this together in order to discuss and peer assess our work so far.

Highlighting their own use of prepositions and looking at examples of their peers' use of prepositions refocused my class on the learning objective. The annotated *Skitch* images provided a visual example of the use of prepositions as sentence openers. This gave me an invaluable insight into their level of understanding about how prepositions can be used.

## Maths lesson

### Capturing learning live

To give another example: in a maths lesson on data handling, I completed a pre-assessment quiz based on a range of SATs (National Curriculum Tests) questions using the *Socrative* app to check the children's level of understanding. This evidence helped me to arrange differentiated groups. I then set the children the task of presenting data through a paper-based data poster, often referred to as an 'infographic', so that I could see that they could construct a purposeful variety of graphs and charts. I asked them talk through this process in pairs and to capture their learning live using the *AudioBoom* app, which records audio and allows it to be saved, edited and uploaded to the internet. This helped to focus their discussions and gave me a chance to catch any learning points I had missed whilst I was working with other children. It also formed the basis for peer-assessment at a later stage in the lesson.

### Reflecting on learning

After their infographics were complete, I asked the children to reflect on their learning. I wanted them to focus on the choices they had made when picking their research question, and to explain why they chose particular graphs to present their data. For this, I used the app *ThingLink*, which allows you to take a photo and add information around it. In this case, the children took a photo of their paper-based infographic and then added voice recordings, videos or just text, on each aspect of their infographic. For example, one piece of information might say 'I used a pie chart to show the main device people used to access the internet as it was clear that this was data from the whole sample.' Reflecting on their learning in this way gave the children independence and flexibility in how they chose to share their thoughts. After they had reflected on their choices, and created an individual record for my assessment, they peer assessed each other's ThingLinks through the shared online account.

## DT lesson

### Ongoing learning maps

Finally, for ongoing projects, tablets provide an opportunity to regularly update a digital artefact to represent a learning journey. In a design and technology (DT) project in which Year 5 made models of a theme park ride, I asked the children to create an ebook using the app *Book Creator*. From the initial group decisions to the annotated photos of the finished working models, the ebooks allowed children to combine text, images, videos and voice recordings to share reflections on their learning.

At the end of each lesson the children thought about what they had achieved, why they made those choices and what they planned to do in the subsequent lesson; they then recorded this in their ebooks. Making each child accountable for their learning in this way gave them a clearer focus. It enabled me to tap into their thinking and to steer them back on track if necessary, as well as helping me to assess their individual contribution to the group work.

# Taking it further

The examples of practice shared here are taken from a number of lessons, but they could also be adapted for any subject, year group or key stage due to the open-ended nature of the apps. For example, when using *Answer Garden* with Year 1 children, you might ask them to list time connectives rather than prepositions.

---

**Activity**

There are several apps that support each stage of the visible learning cycle. Explore some of the apps listed in the table below and compare their use to traditional Assessment for Learning strategies.

---

**Table 3.1** Apps supporting visible learning

| Pre/post assessment | Capturing learning live | Pit stops or mini plenaries | Reflecting on learning | Ongoing learning maps |
|---|---|---|---|---|
| *Answer Garden* (collaborative ideas map) | *SloPro* (slow motion films) | *Socrative* (quick question) | *Socrative: Exit Ticket* (polls and quizzes) | *WordPress* (blogging) |
| *Socrative* (quizzes and polls) | *Video* | *Padlet* (website) (online bulletin board) | *ScreenChomp* (screencasting) | *Book Creator* (making ebooks) |
| *Mindomo* (mindmapping) | *Explain Everything* (screencasting) | *Skitch* (annotating images) | *ThingLink* (making interactive images) | *AudioBoom* (soundrecording) |
| *MindMash* (mindmapping) | *ScreenChomp* (screencasting) | iPad *Mirroring/ Reflector* | *Skitch* (annotating images) | *MindMash* (mindmapping) |
| *Show Me* (screencasting) | *AudioBoom* (soundrecording) | | Photo + Padlet = Discussion | *Mindomo* (mindmapping) |
| *Skitch* (annotating images) | | | *Tagxedo/Word Salad* (word clouds) | |

Add three of these apps into your medium-term planning. Focus on what you are trying to achieve by capturing the learning at each stage of the visible learning cycle. To help with this, consider the following questions:

- Why are you using this app? What does it allow that other methods do not?

- Why is this a good place and time to make the learning explicit? How will capturing learning at this point help progress children's learning?

# Discussion

We will discuss some of the advantages of using these visible learning techniques to inform both teaching and learning behaviours. The focus will be on a comparison between traditional Assessment for Learning (known as AfL or formative assessment) and assessment methods using tablets. We will also consider how tablets can increase metacognition and personalised learning.

## Assessment for Learning (AfL)

As seen in the case study above, there are many potential uses for tablets supporting AfL within the classroom, from pre/post assessments to regular teacher 'check-ins' throughout the learning cycle. Over the last ten years, there have been several initiatives to promote AfL within education (Assessment Reform Group, 2002; Jones, 2005; DCSF, 2008) and, as teachers, we know that AfL is an important aspect of day-to-day teaching. Giving quality feedback and advice on next steps, with differentiated success criteria, makes for high quality teaching that responds to individual needs (Wiliam, 2000). With this in mind, AfL should be a priority within the classroom, but it can be a hard goal to achieve given the time-consuming nature of regularly assessing, marking and feeding back to all children within a class (Antoniou and James, 2014). It is worth exploring ways in which tablets can help to make this process more responsive.

We have seen that the use of tablets alongside more standard teaching methods can offer a range of opportunities, allowing for snapshots of successful learning within our own classrooms as well as quickly highlighting misconceptions so that they can be addressed straight away. The benefits of using technology for assessment have long been recognised (Ravitz, 2002), however, the adoption of assessment techniques is still low across Europe (Redecker, 2013). We will discuss some potential benefits of using tablets and strategies to support AfL within a classroom environment:

1. **Differentiated learning for all**

   One of the simplest ways tablets can be used is to collect instant responses from all children and adjust your teaching as their prior knowledge and needs emerge, whilst keeping the data for a later, deeper, level of analysis. This can enable you to be more flexible in the classroom and it also makes it easier to analyse data to inform future teaching. Analysing work in this way allows teachers to see trends of misunderstandings within their classes, so that they can address them (Beatty and Gerace, 2009).

   If each pupil creates a mindmap of their existing learning, using an app like *Mindomo*, they can add to it at the end of each lesson and send it to their teacher using e-mail or *Dropbox*, which lets you share files over the internet. You can use a keyword search to determine how many children within the class are using the correct terminology, for example 'point' or 'dot' when discussing coordinates in maths.

As well as being useful from a teaching perspective, there is also a direct benefit to learning in terms of the pupils' accountability and anonymity. Using the more standard 'hands up' approach to AfL questioning techniques, many students know that the likelihood of them being picked is minimal and therefore do not challenge themselves with answers. When students know that each of their answers can be traced back to themselves, they make a greater effort to try their best. At the same time, the option of anonymity amongst their peers (due to individual answers being sent directly to the teacher) protects those who may feel more vulnerable answering questions in front of an audience (Roschelle *et al.*, 2004).

In these cases, the *Socrative* and *Answer Garden* apps are good choices. They offer an opportunity to share answers with the class, whilst allowing the anonymity of not pointing out individual children. *Socrative* creates instant graphs showing how many children chose which multiple-choice option, or how many answered 'true/false' questions. *Answer Garden* displays each written answer from a child, but with no identifier as to which child said what. Repeated choices display larger and make them stand out, giving a visual representation of group opinions.

Once you get to grips with the process, you will find that assessing work in a digital format is much more efficient than looking at paper-based work, and is therefore more likely to be carried out by teachers who already have a busy schedule. As well as this, in my opinion, the anonymity offered to less confident learners, and the accountability offered to less motivated learners, is unrivalled by paper-based forms of AfL.

## 2. Immediate feedback

Through real-time questioning with apps like *Socrative*, we can get immediate feedback on children's current levels of understanding with relatively little teacher time required. A quick pre-planned quiz can be completed by children individually and they can each receive immediate feedback as to correct and incorrect answers, including explanations of errors (Peat and Franklin, 2002). Research suggests that this immediacy plays a vital role in the impact that feedback has on the learner. In short (as noted by Nunan, 2010), the sooner, the better!

Beyond the apps already mentioned, another option was the immediacy of children being able to share their ongoing work with their peers. For example, children might use the app *Tagxedo* to create a word cloud of common words, the app *ScreenChomp* to capture their screen and explain what they have been doing, the app *ThingLink* to explain the decisions they had made throughout their work, or the app *Audioboo* to share a conversation or learning discussion. Using these apps, the children could simply and efficiently share their work in progress and gain valuable peer feedback in addition to that of their teacher.

If we were to recreate these scenarios without the aid of tablets it would be a lot more intrusive on the learning environment. We would have to collect everyone's work, display it or hand it out somewhere to ensure that children have the opportunity to preview what other children have done. Tablets help classes collaborate and grow into local learning communities by syncing the processes of producing and responding in this way.

### 3. Peer- and self-assessment

Good assessment means helping children to think about their learning and what decisions they could make to improve it, and helping them to share their developing understanding with their peers (Jones, 2005). Features of good feedback practice suggested by Nicol and Macfarlane-Dick (2006) include self-assessment, and teacher and peer dialogue. Willey and Gardner (2009) found that, when using technology to ensure simple and frequent use of self- and peer-assessment, learners achieved the desired learning outcomes. This was supported by a literature review which found that children giving feedback on their peers' work often led to a larger number of improvements in their own work (Hepplestone *et al.*, 2011). Managing this as a classroom teacher is a careful job, as you do not want those who struggle to feel self-conscious about the work they are sharing, and you want those who are achieving well to learn from assessing their peers' work (Jones, 2005).

Examples of peer- and self-assessment are mentioned above in the 'Reflecting on Learning' section of the learning cycle (Figure 3.1). Here, children have the opportunity to take their existing work and annotate it with apps such as *ScreenChomp* (an app where you can make a narrated screencast), *ThingLink* (an app where you can annotate an image with text, video and sound) or *Skitch* (an app where you can annotate an image with text, arrows and highlights. The experience of explaining learning encourages children to reflect on objectives and success criteria, and refocuses their attention on the task.

Once children have created these digital artefacts describing their self-assessment, they can easily be shared either through websites such as *Padlet*, a virtual wall which allows students to post images, videos and text, or simply through a shared log-in account for an app. I tend to take this opportunity to encourage dialogic teaching by asking children to discuss someone else's work with their partner, and be ready to feedback positives and suggestions to the class.

Overall, the use of tablets to encourage self-assessment has benefits over regular assessment methods because it uses work that children have already created as a starting point. From here, children can add reasoning and explanations whilst easily referring to their own work. As well as this, the multimedia aspect of using tablets is likely to engage a wider range of students, as those who are less comfortable with text can share their thoughts using narration, video or images. Learners with a wide range of abilities can create impressive digital artefacts using various combinations of these media. Finally, by making annotated assessments students leave their original work intact so that any errors made in their own understanding and explanations can be used as evidence by the teacher without deleting or defacing the originals.

From a peer-assessment perspective, the use of tablets allows for an agile distribution of children's work. This means that only a small amount of time needs to be used physically sharing the work and the majority can be spent having the assessment conversations. As well as this, letting the children view everyone's work brings us back to the idea of accountability, as, even if work is anonymous, students will recognise who put in the most effort. Finally, a larger range of skills and focused conversations occur if you can encourage children to analyse and discuss a range of different examples of work. For example, if you ask children to find a piece of writing that creates the strongest visual image, the children will spend time reading through several examples and discussing their thoughts with their partners. Add to this that they must give three reasons for their choice, and you have a range of high-level processing skills being used.

## Individual needs

As well as the numerous AfL benefits that are provided by tablets, there is also an opportunity for us to ensure that we meet the individual needs of children within the class: from being able to offer specific children an alternative pre-assessment quiz, to being able to offer children the opportunity to complete learning tasks in a way that allows them to express themselves as individuals.

The need to address individual needs has been highlighted by Brunvand and Byrd (2011), who explored the use of the website and app *VoiceThread* by individuals within a class. They found that this tool provided a guided learning environment which met individual needs and learning styles, and enabled a range of children to feel success. This supports the idea that using open-ended visible learning apps such as *Book Creator* (for making ebooks using a combination of text, photos, videos and audio), *MindMash* (an app which allows you to combine several different types of media to organise like a notebook) and *Mindomo* (a mind mapping app that allows you to include different media in connected webs) can allow your learners to communicate and share their learning more readily than with pen and paper methods.

## Metacognition

Metacognition is described as 'awareness and understanding of one's own thought processes' (Oxford Dictionary), and research suggests that metacognitive skills can predict learning outcomes (Veenman and Spaans, 2005). Veenman and Spaans' study goes on to explore the idea that, within education, 'young students should be instructed to acquire metacognitive skills in various domains and, subsequently, to apply those skills across the boundaries of tasks and domains' (p173). The 'Reflecting on Learning' and 'Ongoing Learning Maps' stages of the learning cycle mentioned in Figure 3.1 meet this criteria.

Using tablets to encourage learners to recognise and understand their learning increases their understanding as well as their motivation on specific tasks across the curriculum (Liu and Carless, 2006). Reflection is itself a learning experience for children, and tablets offer both teachers and learners interactive insight into the learning as it is happening. Finally, at primary level, metacognition has been used as an intervention where reflection on the learning process develops skills that can be transferred to other learning situations (Dignath and Büttner, 2008).

## Self-regulation and self-efficacy

With the surge of technological development taking place over the last 20 years, the idea of lifelong learning is now more within our sights than ever before. As teachers, we need to ensure that the children in our classes are best prepared to learn both within and beyond our classroom walls, and tablets are a great way to encourage this. Previously, education was limited by children accessing textbooks, or other school equipment, which was unavailable in their homes. Modelling a positive use of tablets in education can go some way towards resolving this, although we need to take account of the need for equality of access. Ofcom (2013) reported that, in their 2013 survey, 51 per cent of 5–15-year-olds now had home tablet access and that use of a tablet computer at home by the same age group had tripled since the previous year.

Using tablets to make learning visible offers a unique opportunity to allow children to practise strategies such as metacognition and improve self-regulation and self-efficacy in an already full curriculum. Their use has been shown to be beneficial to learning at both primary and secondary level (Dignath and Büttner, 2008). Giving children the choice of how to present their learning can be the first step towards them becoming self-regulated learners who are aware of their own abilities. This coincides with offering them opportunities to reflect on their practice and self-assess their progress (Nicol and Macfarlane-Dick, 2006).

Tablets allow students to present their work in a range of different media, whilst still making it easier for teachers to collate and offer feedback on the work their learners have produced. Giving children greater ownership over their learning helps them to self-regulate and set themselves achievable goals. They need to consider how they are going to show you that they have understood the learning. Alongside this, your children must believe in what they can achieve, as they are the ones being asked to share. In the end, all learning stems from the learners and it is facilitated by the use of tablets to accommodate individual perspectives.

If we think back to the design and technology (DT) lesson discussed previously in this chapter, we have a clear example of a controllable way to manage giving children an open-ended task. The tablets were used alongside DT, and, by using the tablet in this way (showing skills of self-regulation, self-efficacy and metacognition), the children had a clearer understanding of the relevant DT concepts. This is supported by research suggesting that combining spoken text and images allows for deeper understanding (Mayer and Moreno, 2002). Spending just 5–10 minutes at the end of a lesson, reflecting on what the children had achieved, verbalising what they'd learned and planning their next steps, ensured that, as a teacher, I could clearly see the learning that was happening, but, more importantly, so could the children themselves.

## Pedagogy

To ensure that these techniques have the greatest impact on learning in the classroom, you need to ensure that the ethos of this type of assessment and learning is understood by your students. This is not as challenging as it may seem; modelling to children the positive benefits of this type of assessment of learning, rather than on 'marking' them, will help children have a vested interest in this type of activity. Drawing positive attention to those children who are completing tasks effectively and using information to form their learning will reinforce your learning and assessment ethos. Repeatedly returning to, and reminding children, of this assessment process will ensure that they recognise it as a useful learning tool themselves (Keppell *et al.*, 2006).

Recent guidance from the European Union focused on 'The Use of ICT for Assessment ... ' (Redecker, 2013) and has a section specifically relating to pedagogical strategies, stating that teachers should:

- choose assessment formats that encourage alternative solutions and promote experimentation;
- promote self-regulated learning through self- and peer-assessment;
- use ICT-based assessment as a means of making these more innovative learning strategies more readily available.

This supports the above-mentioned strategies to ensure that we are best suiting the needs of our class to create better learning environments, in turn ensuring that everyone reaches their maximum potential.

---

### Activity

Rank the following statements about using tablets for visible learning in order of importance to you.

**Table 3.2**  Ranking about using tablets of visible learning

| Rank | Statements – How important is it to you to: |
|---|---|
| | Collect AfL data from every child |
| | Get feedback from children immediately to check understanding |
| | Allow students to submit their learning in their own medium |
| | Give children an opportunity to recognise their own learning and progress |
| | Allocate opportunities for children to take control of capturing their own learning |

Identify the three next steps you would need to take in order to begin to implement this approach in your classroom.

1. _____

2. _____

3. _____

## Summary and Key Points

We have looked at how tablets can help capture learning through film, photos, screencasts and spoken explanations, making learning visible to both learners and teachers. By using apps, teachers can dip into the learning journey regularly, with minimal disruption to the students. As well as this, the use of tablets can reduce the time spent on assessment and allow more time to give the learners quality feedback.

The visible learning cycle suggested in this chapter focuses attention on the variety of opportunities for teachers to capture learning and make it visible throughout a unit of work. It is unlikely that you would use each of these techniques in every unit, but it is important to recognise each stage individually so that it can be appropriately planned into the curriculum. Whilst little discrete time needs to be given to these activities, as with any assessment, planning and preparation are required to ensure that the maximum impact is achieved.

We focused our discussion on the following advantages of using tablets for AfL over more traditional methods: the simplicity of collecting data from all students; the immediacy of offering feedback to those students; and the ease with which self- and peer-assessment opportunities can be managed within the classroom. From here, we explored extended opportunities for using tablets to deepen learning through visible learning activities that meet the needs of individual students, encourage metacognitive reflections and promote self-regulation within students.

Remember that these strategies are to be used alongside 'traditional' classroom lessons and that the role of the tablet is to capture the learning that is already happening, often in a more subtle way. In the digital age, with tablets playing an increasingly more prominent role in everyday life, we want to equip our students with a range of skills allowing them to harness this technology in their journey to becoming lifelong learners. Bringing learning to the forefront of the lesson has benefits for both the children and the teacher and ensures that our learners are at the heart of their own learning experiences.

## Useful Links

http://ipad4schools.org (accessed 20 December 2014).

Richard Wells' blog looking at the iPads and learning.

http://swaygrantham.co.uk/?s=ipad (accessed 20 December 2014).

Sway Grantham's blog documenting iPad use in her own classroom.

www.unity.com.au/pad201 (accessed 20 December 2014).

Exploring iPads and Bloom's taxonomy.

http://ictevangelist.com/?s=ipad (accessed 20 December 2014).

iPad blog from ICT Evangelist Mark Anderson.

## App List for the Chapter

iPad apps: *Answer Garden, SloPro, Socrative, WordPress, Video, ScreenChomp, Book Creator, Mindomo, Explain Everything, Skitch, ThingLink, Audioboo, MindMash, Reflector, Show Me, Word Salad, VoiceThread*

Android apps: *Socrative, WordPress, Video, Book Creator, Mindomo, Explain Everything, Skitch, ThingLink, Audioboo*

Windows apps: *Socrative*, *Skitch*, *Explain Everything*, *Audioboo*

Web-based tools: *Answer Garden*, *Socrative*, *Mindomo*, *Audioboo*, *ThingLink*, *Tagxedo*, *WordPress*, *VoiceThread*

## Further Reading

The Use of ICT for the Assessment of Key Competencies. **http://ftp.jrc.es/EURdoc/JRC76971.pdf** (accessed 20 December 2014).

A practical guide to the use of ICT in the classroom written for the European Union.

Formative Assessment with iPad: Representing the Process of Learning by Tom Foster as part of the Apple Distinguished Educator 'One Best Thing' series ebook. Includes discussion and classroom examples.

iPads in the classroom: embedding technology in the primary curriculum. A *Guardian* article with a case study of a Year 6 class using iPads to support learning. **http://bit.ly/ipad-primary-curriculum** (accessed 20 December 2014).

## References

Antoniou, P and James, M (2014) Exploring formative assessment in primary school classrooms: Developing a framework of actions and strategies. *Educational Assessment, Evaluation and Accountability*, 26(2), 153–76.

Assessment Reform Group (2002) Assessment for Learning: 10 Principles. Available from: **www.aaia.org. uk/content/uploads/2010/06/Assessment-for-Learning-10-principles.pdf** (accessed 11 August 2014).

Beatty, ID and Gerace, WJ (2009) Technology-enhanced formative assessment: A research-based pedagogy for teaching science with classroom response technology. *Journal of Science Education and Technology*, 18(2), 146–62.

Brunvand, S and Byrd, S (2011) Using VoiceThread to promote learning engagement and success for all students. *Teaching Exceptional Children*. 43(4), 28–37. Available from: **http://voicethread.com/media/ misc/support/JTECVoiceThread.pdf** (accessed 13 August, 2014).

DCSF (2008) The Assessment for Learning Strategy. Department for Children, Schools and Families.

Dignath, C and Büttner, G (2008) Components of fostering self-regulated learning among students: A meta-analysis on intervention studies at primary and secondary school level. *Metacognition and Learning*, 3, 231–64.

Hepplestone, S, Holden, G, Irwin, B, Parkin, HJ and Thorpe, L (2011) Using technology to encourage student engagement with feedback: A literature review. *Research in Learning Technology*, 19(2), 117–27.

Jones, CA (2005) *Assessment for Learning*. London: Learning and Skills Development Agency.

Keppell, M, Au, E, Ma, A and Chan, C (2006) Peer learning and learning-oriented assessment in technology-enhanced environments. *Assessment and Evaluation in Higher Education*, 31, 453–64.

Liu, N-F and Carless, D (2006) Peer feedback: The learning element of peer assessment. *Teaching in Higher Education*, 11(3), 279–90.

Mayer, RE and Moreno, R (2002) Aids to computer-based multimedia learning. *Learning and Instruction*, 12(1), 107–19.

Nicol, DJ and Macfarlane-Dick, D (2006) Formative assessment and self-regulated learning: A model and seven principles of good feedback practice. *Studies in Higher Education*, 31(2), 199–218.

Nunan, D (2010) *Technology Supports for Second Language Learning, International Encyclopedia of Education* (3rd ed., Vol. 8, pp. 204–9). Oxford: Elsevier.

Ofcom (2013) *Children and Parents: Media Use and Attitudes Report*. Available from: **http://stakeholders. ofcom.org.uk/binaries/research/media-literacy/october-2013/research07Oct2013.pdf** (accessed 20 August 2014).

Ravitz, J (2002) CILT2000: Using technology to support ongoing formative assessment in the classroom. *Journal of Science Education and Technology*, 11(3), 293–96.

Redecker, C (2013) *The Use of ICT for the Assessment of Key Competencies*. Luxembourg: Publications Office of the European Union. Available from: **http://ftp.jrc.es/EURdoc/JRC76971.pdf** (accessed 13 August 2014).

Roschelle, J, Abrahamson, LA and Penuel, WR (2004) Integrating classroom network technology and learning theory to improve classroom science learning: A literature synthesis. Paper presented at the Annual Meeting of the American Educational Research Association, San Diego.

Veenman, MVJ and Spaans, MA (2005) Relation between intellectual and metacognitive skills: Age and task differences. *Learning and Individual Differences*, 15, 159–76.

Wiliam, D (2000) Integrating Summative and Formative Functions of Assessment. Keynote address to the European Association for Educational Assessment, Prague: Czech Republic.

# Chapter 4

# Talk and collaboration

## Introduction

This chapter explores ways in which the creative use of tablet apps can promote talk and collaboration within classrooms. The case study will focus on games-based learning approaches to curriculum development, utilising apps and other digital tools to develop game design skills and understanding. The ways in which this can promote discussion and active reflection will be considered and the case study also explores using technology to support the writing process as a cross-curricular project with a Year 6 class. The chapter discussion attempts to frame the case study examples with reflection on academic approaches to thinking, dialogue and pedagogy.

### Learning Objectives

At the end of this chapter you should be able to:

- design programs that accomplish specific goals;
- be confident and creative users of information and communication technology;
- use spoken language to develop understanding through exploring ideas, participating in discussions and considering and evaluating different viewpoints, attending to and building on the contribution of others.

### Links to Teachers' Standards

The following Teachers' Standards are particularly relevant to this chapter:

TS1 Set goals that stretch and challenge pupils of all backgrounds, abilities and dispositions.
TS2 Demonstrate knowledge and understanding of how pupils learn and how this impacts on teaching.
TS2 Encourage pupils to take a responsible and conscientious attitude to their own work and study.
TS3 Have a secure knowledge of the relevant subject(s) and curriculum areas, foster and maintain pupils' interest in the subject and address misunderstandings.
TS4 Contribute to the design and provision of an engaging curriculum within the relevant subject area(s).

TS5 Know when and how to differentiate appropriately, using approaches that enable pupils to be taught effectively.

TS6 Give pupils regular feedback, both orally and through accurate marking, and encourage them to respond to the feedback.

## Links to National Curriculum Programmes of Study

### Key Stage 1 and Key Stage 2

- Pupils become digitally literate – able to use, and express themselves and develop their ideas through information and communication technology – at a level suitable for the future workplace and as active participants in a digital world.
- Pupils use technology purposefully to create, organise, store, manipulate and retrieve digital content.
- Pupils select, use and combine a variety of software (including internet services) on a range of digital devices to design and create a range of programs, systems and content that accomplish given goals, including collecting, analysing, evaluating and presenting data and information.

# Example from practice

## Context

**In the classroom**

The opportunities for learning through the use of digital gaming are diverse and massive. The speed and ease with which basic game development can be achieved using apps such as *Sketch Nation* can provide a platform for outstanding cross-curricular projects and really make an impact on progress, standards and pupil independence. This chapter describes one project (Upper Key Stage 2), which could easily be adapted to suit Key Stage 1 and which could support almost any topic/subject. A core aspect of this approach was to develop pedagogy to support rich talk and collaboration – promoting thinking and deep reflection.

This case study, entitled 'Game Designers', was a week-long project focusing on ways of raising standards in writing by using a game creation app as a stimulus for a persuasive writing task.

The initial objective of the project was to design, produce and promote a game based on an element of our current topic. In class some of the children wanted to link the game to last term's World War II topic, but most chose to base their game on the new topic of African wildlife and diversity. The whole outline of the project was shared with the children at the outset so they could plan and organise their work. The basic requirements were that the pupils would need to: design and produce an original game; collect video and voice recorded feedback from their peers – reflect on this feedback and make appropriate improvements; create a persuasive and informative marketing display on their learning wall; write an advert for their game as if it appeared in the App Store; create online multimedia promotional material on their blog space; and present and try to sell their game to a class of Year 5 pupils at a showcase event. This would lead to the culmination of what was ultimately a business and enterprise project.

## Outline

This case study outlines a number of key features of a sequence of lessons and learning events that took place within this project. The features are all important components of the sequence and they provided essential 'building blocks' for the development of the children's learning and understanding.

## Game design

The free app *Sketch Nation* was introduced to the children. It is a quick-to-learn and easy-to-use game design app, which allows users to produce their own unique digital game.

The children were told that they would be designing a game for Year 5 pupils. The project would also involve making a persuasive digital poster, movie adverts with a backing track and a persuasive piece of writing to advertise the game in the App Store.

After a brief demonstration the pupils were put into pairs and were encouraged to discuss and explore the features of the app and begin to think about the game they wanted to design. After deciding the genre of the game, the pupils were encouraged to design a prototype in *Simple Mode*. The name, player, platform and background all had to be unique and not exactly like games they might have played before.

## Feedback

After a few minutes of designing their prototype game the pupils were asked to share their games amongst their peers. They were asked to collect oral/video feedback on their tablet. This could be collected using the app *Book Creator*. The pupils were encouraged to find the answers to following types of questions: Are the graphics appealing? Is this game challenging enough? Will the theme of the game appeal to pupils in Year 5? What improvements could they make? After they had collected it, they were asked to listen to their feedback and record, either as a video or as a voice recording, what they had done well and how they were going to make improvements to their game.

Reflecting on their feedback, pupils were introduced to the advanced mode in *Sketch Nation*, in which you can control every aspect of the game. Pupils were able to design their own characters, a range of obstacles and enemies, and platforms and backgrounds to suit the type of game they wanted to achieve. It is possible to create graphical content in the app by scanning in artwork or using downloaded and edited images. The amount of content that can be developed is vast. Scoring systems, power-ups, frequency of obstacles, effects of collisions and so many more features are all completely editable. The quality of the completed games was excellent. Some were extremely challenging, some were fun and some were a little easy. In a short space of time, the children produced exactly what they wanted.

## Preparing the promotional material

Linking back to previous work on persuasive writing, pupils researched different types of advertising and features of branding and promotion. They were able to create their own display on their learning wall, using their own content. Every aspect of their work was also posted to their own blog space.

## Learning walls

The classroom learning walls were an integral part of the 'Game Design Project' and many other projects that we covered in Year 6.

Learning walls are spaces in the classroom; they are divided into equally-sized sections, with a space allocated to each child. Their purpose is to allow pupils to experiment with presenting work for an audience, to develop a sense of ownership of a publicly viewable space and to develop skills in giving and receiving relevant and valid feedback.

Once work has been completed it is displayed on the wall and previous work is taken down and kept in a scrapbook, having been photographed and displayed on the pupil's own blog space. The children managed the wall completely and decided on content, layout and any additional or interactive elements. The wall remains the first point of display for a large proportion of work produced in class. Sticky notes are used by pupils and staff to provide constructive comments and feedback.

It has been important to stress to pupils, parents and school staff that the children are responsible for the content displayed on their own wall space. In many ways, the wall has become an interactive learning tool as well as a place to showcase work. The pupils are very aware that if high standards are not maintained, this will be pointed out by any number of visitors to their wall.

The power of preparing work for an audience has promoted independence and creativity in many of the pupils. The children enjoy giving and receiving feedback, and many staff, including the head teacher, regularly inspect the wall and give suggestions for improvement or recognition of excellent work. A large number of parents have already been to view their child's wall and parent feedback suggests that children are discussing their school work a lot more at home.

## Titles and logos

Following research in the App Store, the pupils designed their own app logos and titles, using classroom stationery and thinking carefully about colour schemes and a consistent style for their branding.

## Digital posters

Posters were made in *Strip Designer* – a powerful tool which can create high quality work. They were asked to take a number of screenshots from the game, such as the game play, main characters, enemies, power-ups, special effects etc., to create their persuasive poster. In pairs, they discussed and added the name of the game, persuasive words and phrases (such as rhetorical questions), cost and feedback from their peers. Once complete, the poster was saved to the camera roll.

## Video adverts

The image created in *Strip Designer* (the persuasive poster) was applied to the background in the app *Tellagami*. The pupils used the image to make a recording in order to present their ideas orally, using persuasive techniques. It was explained that this would form part of an advert used to persuade their audience to play the game. Using the background created in *Strip Designer* provided the pupils with a visual prompt, which helped them think about sequence and rehearse the language they would using in their writing. The pupils were restricted to 30 seconds of recording, so they were encouraged to rehearse their ideas with a partner before recording their persuasive advert. This was saved to the camera roll to be edited and used in their final advert in *iMovie*.

Pupils filmed each other playing their games so that they could capture examples of the excitement produced during the game play. The videos were then airdropped back to the pupils iPads. They also captured video testimonials from their peers to add to their final advert.

*iMovie* was used to make the advertisements (using *Tellagami*, game play and testimonials). This allowed easy editing and a combination of images, video, captions and titles. Soundtracks were created in *GarageBand*. The 'smart' composition aspect of this app, along with the excellent drum machine and sampling features, make it easy to compose effective music to suit any purpose. It doesn't take a specialist to produce high quality original compositions with *GarageBand*.

## QR Codes

Each pupil has their own unique QR Code, which links to their own blog space on the Year 6 blog. An app called *QRafter Pro* was used to create the QR Codes. Each time a pupil has posted work to their blog space, which is relevant to the theme of the wall, the pupil can use a QR Code on their learning wall space. The pupils are invited to visit each others' wall space and scan the QR Codes – using *Scan app* – and leave comments about the post on their blog space. If a comment has been left, the children are encouraged to reply.

## Presenting to an audience

As the culmination to this project, the children from the adjacent classroom (Year 5) were invited to a New Games Launch Event. The visiting pupils viewed the learning walls, engaged in discussions with game designers, scanned the QR codes to view the online content and had the chance to test the games. Each visitor had five game tokens and was able to 'purchase' their favourite games. This session was focused, very interactive and proved to be an exceptional opportunity for promoting speaking and listening, questioning and answering. It also provided valuable feedback to the pupils on the quality of their game designs and promotional material.

## Cross-curricular links

Each pupil's starting point was a history or geography objective, such as: 'Demonstrate an understanding of the main threats to wildlife in Africa' or 'Recognise the implications on the Battle of Britain in WWII.' The opportunities to expand learning in a project like this are numerous. There were many opportunities for writing in terms of persuasive texts, summarising feedback and reporting on the New Games Launch Event. During the event, records of scores were kept for each player of the game, allowing investigations into averages and data handling opportunities.

There was a significant impact on the pupil's ability to orally present and explain their work using appropriate styles and vocabulary. The integrated use of tablet technology had allowed tablets to become a tool to support and enhance learning. The pupils only use it when it is needed and will often choose other methods of presentation and research.

# Discussion

The case study examples within this chapter provide ideas for creative uses of technology to promote talk and collaboration. A number of key iPad apps are discussed, as well as wider pedagogical tools and techniques to enhance learning. A case study of this nature enables understanding of how one teacher has approached the development of an inclusive, technology-rich learning environment. Developing environments with 'rich' talk and collaboration is an important feature of primary classrooms.

## Talk and collaboration

A number of studies have developed our understanding of how talk and collaboration can develop children's learning. Collaborative learning approaches can often be seen as indicators of successful classrooms (Littleton and Mercer, 2013; Slavin, 2009). The nature of these collaborative environments is such that 'transferable' thinking and related reasoning and communication skills are seen as being natural developments. However Littleton and Mercer (2013) also indicate that 'collaborative learning', often seen as group work, may not always be as productive as hoped. Unstructured discussion and group work without adequate purpose and direction will, unsurprisingly, not have an impact on learning. Children need great direction and skill development to be able to ensure that their talk and collaboration lead to 'good' learning.

The examples of use of technology within this chapter attempt to show purposeful tasks situated within engaging contexts which provide good engagement for pupils. Indeed some indicators of successful collaborative environments identify the 'dual role' of being teacher and learner, something enabled by designing tasks which ensure that learners take the role of designing learning and information provision for others:

> *Collaboration includes taking the perspectives of both the student as learner and the teacher and assumes that group problem solving leads to greater success than working alone.*

> (Garton, 2007, p197)

Indeed Staarman (2009) identifies a range of ways of approaching computer-mediated collaboration and communication within primary literacy teaching. Within her study, the nature of cognitive and regulatory discourse is analysed to provide a greater understanding of the complexities of approaching collaborative group work using technology.

## Thinking and dialogue

Chapter 5 of this book, iPads in the Early Years, presents some ideas on how technology has been discussed in relation to thinking and dialogue. A range of studies identify the importance of shared use of technology to promote dialogue and resultant thinking. Stanton and Neale (2003) explore the potential of shared computer usage to generate collaboration, both in thinking and in dialogue.

Technological environments provide a number of features, such as engaging animation and multimodal displays of information, which promote discussion and talk and demonstrate 'rich' cognitive processes. Wild (2011) identified the impact of the shared use of computers on the thinking of pairs of 5- and 6-year-olds. Specific benefits rested particularly on the supplementary role of computers alongside other professionals' work with children; where adults could not always give attention to children, the computer allowed the continued development of thinking.

### Multimodalities and iPads

A key feature of a number of the case study examples provided within this chapter is a 'rich' multimodal environment. Apps such as *GarageBand*, *iMovie*, *Sketch Nation* and *Strip Designer* allow children to easily incorporate images and audio to creatively portray information in a range of ways. Discussions in other chapters of this book have focused on the impact of tablet-enabled multimodal communication – this has great potential impact on learning and is easily allowed by tablet environments. Investigations of talk and collaboration using the benefits of recent mobile technologies are not fully developed. Many studies have focused on talk and collaboration using desktop and 'fixed' environments, which neglect many of the features of using mobile technologies – namely the easy and immediate incorporation of a range of images and audio.

Recent studies are beginning to identify some of the benefits of particular apps. Talk and collaboration enabled by apps such as *Explain Everything* are identified by Wise *et al.* (in press) in a study of iPad use in science investigations:

> *Using the iPads to video and review happenings closely appeared to really help develop observational skills and pique curiosity. Using the multimodality of the iPad to record as results, annotate findings, add images and allow video to be combined in one place worked particularly well for 'mixing' as the process often happened quite quickly (e.g.: food colouring dissolving in water). Being able to revisit the dissolution processes via video also supported the children developing a more exact, accurate and detailed explanation of what actually happened.*

> (Wise *et al.*, in press)

Certainly, tablet apps enable children to quickly capture their ideas in a range of ways. They allow easy editing and playback and enable greater evidence and record-keeping of processes that can be used later within learning. Within maths and science investigations, this is particularly important as reflection on processes has often relied on pupils' memory and scant notes. With the accurate recording of processes, and later playback, children can easily recall what happened and then reflect on this, leading to greater opportunity for talk and collaboration and, subsequently, more developed learning.

## Useful Links

**www.mrandrewsonline.com** (accessed 20 December 2014).

**www.mrandrewsonline.blogspot.com** (accessed 20 December 2014).

## App List for the Chapter

*iMovie, Skitch, App Store, GarageBand, Strip Designer, Sketch Nation, Tellagami, Qrafter, Scan.*

## References

Garton, AF (2007) Learning through collaboration, in Salili, F and Hoosain, R (eds) *Culture, Motivation and Learning: A Multicultural Perspective.* Greenwich, CT: Information Age Publishing.

Littleton, K and Mercer, N (2013) *Interthinking: Putting Talk to Work.* London: Routledge

Slavin, R (2009) Cooperative learning, in McCulloch, G and Crook, D (eds) *International Encyclopedia of Education.* London: Routledge

Staarman, JK (2009) Collaboration and technology: The nature of discourse in primary school computer-supported collaborative learning practices. University of Nijmegen Thesis. Available from: **http://education.exeter.ac.uk/download.php?id=1440** (accessed 15 October 2014).

Stanton, D and Neale, HR (2003) The effects of multiple mice on children's talk and interaction. *Journal of Computer Assisted Learning*, 19, 229–38.

Wild, M (2011) Thinking together: Exploring aspects of shared thinking between young children during a computer-based literacy task. *International Journal of Early Years Education*, 19, 3–4, 219–23.

Wise, N, McGregor, D and Bird, JC (in press) Reflections from a year four classroom: Impact of iPads to help children think scientifically. *Primary Science.*

# Chapter 5

# iPads in the Early Years

## Introduction

This chapter focuses on the use of iPads within the Early Years Foundation Stage (EYFS). It includes a number of short examples of using iPads in a variety of ways – both as pedagogical and administrative tools. The use of tablets, and specifically iPads, in the EYFS is perhaps less developed than in other areas of primary schools. Part of the reason for this may stem from teachers' philosophical stance on the place of technology within EYFS settings – this issue, alongside suggestions for the mitigation of concerns about early technology, are included within the discussion.

---

### Learning Objectives

At the end of this chapter you should be able to:

- identify a number of apps for use within the Early Years Foundation Stage;
- understand how these apps can be integrated within the EYFS curriculum and assessment;
- apply some of these ideas to create and assess engaging activities for children in the EYFS.

---

### Links to Teachers' Standards

The following Teachers' Standards are particularly relevant to this chapter:

TS1 Establish a safe and stimulating environment for pupils.
Set goals that stretch and challenge pupils of all backgrounds, abilities and dispositions.
TS2 Demonstrate knowledge and understanding of how pupils learn and how this impacts on teaching.
Encourage pupils to take a responsible and conscientious attitude to their own work and study.
TS3 Foster and maintain pupils' interest in the subject, and address misunderstandings.
TS4 Promote a love of learning and children's intellectual curiosity.
Contribute to the design and provision of an engaging curriculum within the relevant subject area(s).
TS5 Have a clear understanding of the needs of all pupils, including those with special educational needs; those of high ability; those with English as an additional language; those with disabilities; and be able to use and evaluate distinctive teaching approaches to engage and support them.

## Links to EYFS Early Learning Goals

### Understanding the world

Technology: children recognise that a range of technology is used in places such as homes and schools. They select and use technology for particular purposes.

### Expressive arts and design

Exploring and using media and materials: children sing songs, make music and dance, and experiment with ways of changing these. They safely use and explore a variety of materials, tools and techniques, experimenting with colour, design, texture, form and function.

### Being imaginative

Children use what they have learnt about media and materials in original ways, thinking about uses and purposes.

# Examples from practice

In this chapter, we have included a number of different ways in which tablets have been used within the EYFS. These include specific educational experiences and activities, as well as the administrative use of tablets to aid assessment and tracking of pupil progress. For each example, we have included a brief overview of the context of the activities together with information about the approach and specific apps that were used.

**In the classroom**

## *Ongoing continuous provision*

### Context

This short case study gives an overview of an approach to provide access to iPads during continuous provision sessions within the Foundation Stage unit of a small four-class primary school. A number of iPads have been purchased for use across the school and also to develop iPad awareness and use amongst the youngest children. The Foundation Stage class usually has between 10 and 15 children enjoying learning in a purpose-built outside classroom (a cosy, vibrant, ski-style chalet).

### Outline

The school decided to develop iPad use in the Foundation Stage class to provide early skills and awareness in using touch-screen environments before more developed use in Key Stage 1 and Key Stage 2. The head teacher and the Foundation Stage teacher, in discussion with the creative ideas of a consultant from an educational technical support firm, decided to provide a fixed point of access to iPads, using wall-mounted brackets (**www.ram-mount.co.uk**).

The class teacher provides access to the iPads during 'choosing time', continuous provision sessions. Children are able to access a range of phonics, maths, drawing, photo, art and puzzle apps (a list of the apps used in this class is included at the end of the chapter). The class teacher and teaching assistant (TA) carefully monitor access to the iPads. They ensure that the children only access the iPads for up to 20 minutes at a time and access appropriate apps, and they guide some of the activities that the children undertake.

This nature of access ensures that children have regular and frequent access to the apps. They are then able to develop skills over a period of time and will frequently involve their friends in their learning and activities. The fixed access points also ensure calm and considered access to the iPads – children can see when they are available and will negotiate when they can use the iPad. The teacher monitors use and will sometimes decide to have 'iPad-free' days – to control access and guide children to other focused activities. The iPads can be easily clipped in and out of the mount fixings, leading to flexibility in use and secure storage/charging at the end of the school day. The teacher also decided not to allow wireless access to the internet – thus mitigating any e-safety issues with inappropriate contact and content.

The teacher chooses a restricted range of about 15–20 apps. This is a generic set of art, phonics, early maths and creative apps. However, apps that relate to the current curriculum focus or topic can also be provided. Children are involved in deciding which apps can be used and develop skills in choosing and justifying which apps are useful for their learning. This approach has allowed the children to develop their own approaches to using the iPads. Different cohorts have had different relationships with using the tablet environment – this has usually been due to the nature of experience that the children have with tablet use outside school. For instance, the previous cohort was keen to use the photo and video iPad software to develop stories, add music and perform for each other. The current cohort is more focused on games and activities, such as puzzles, maths quizzes and art apps.

## iPads as an observational tool

### Context

As part of an ongoing action point in the school development plan, this mid-sized rural primary school has a focus on developing assessment methods in its Foundation Stage class. There is one Foundation Stage class in the school. It consists of 27 children, and has a single entry in September of each year. There are three staff members attached to the class: one class teacher and two TAs. A substantial investment in technology – purchasing 60 iPads for use across the school – has been made. The strategic plan for the implementation of these devices focused on EYFS assessment as having the most educational impact for this age range.

### Outline

Initial discussions amongst EYFS staff identified the intuitive nature of the camera and video tools for easily recording children's learning behaviours. Each staff member received an iPad mini and used it to take still and video images of the children, which were then used for playback and discussion as part of team meetings and assessment recording. These recordings were particularly useful in analysing the development of children's language and they allowed assessments to be made with fewer observations.

As staff confidence and adeptness in the use of the iPads developed, they began to seek out ways of developing their assessment practices. A next step was to look for note taking apps, which would allow ways of sorting evidence and combining photo, textual and audio notes. The staff eventually decided to develop their skills in using *Evernote*, as it allowed easy tagging and access to information using a range of web-based platforms. They decided to have one *Evernote* account for the EYFS staff – they all shared the same username and password and were then able to create records for each note they were writing about the children in the EYFS.

An important part of the process was the development of tags and tagging for the notes they created. As they created a note – which was a record of a particular learning event or episode – they were then easily able to tag (tagging is a way of archiving and storing information for easy recall using tag searching) using children's names, effective learning characteristics and learning aspects (based on the revised EYFS framework). An important initial resource was a blog record from another teacher who had implemented this approach: **www.simonhaughton.co.uk/2013/03/using-evernote-for-eyfs-observations.html**.

The EYFS team quickly identified the benefits of tablet use, which enabled note taking using a range of different ways of communicating (text, audio, images and video). The *Evernote* app easily allows integration and categorising of a range of notes – which can be linked together to provide a thorough record of particular learning events and episodes. By recording a particular episode and then tagging with multiple children's names, teachers were able to quickly build a well-rounded picture of learning across the EYFS.

At the start of 2014, the EYFS teacher was introduced to an EYFS note taking and recording app called *2Simple 2Build a Profile*. As with *Evernote*, this app was able to quickly record, multimodally, learning events and observations of children in the EYFS. The EYFS staff also identified a number of other benefits, including the easy creation of pupil accounts, a more intuitive tagging and tag retrieval system and easy ways of sharing information by e-mail and the web management system. The most important feature of the app was the ability to cross-reference learning observations with the EYFS framework. After recording a learning event and tagging with a child or children's names, the app is designed to allow staff to search for and then choose the appropriate age band and area of learning from the EYFS framework.

The EYFS staff in this school discussed how using tablets for note taking has positively impacted on children's learning. A main advantage has been the ability to record and retrieve a larger quantity and wider range of learning events. Rapid recall of observation – easily cross-referenced to the EYFS framework – has enabled staff to begin planning learning experiences focused on a wider range of individual needs. By removing time spent on sorting and filing paper records – as well as completing handwritten notes matched to the EYFS framework – the staff can spend more time assessing behaviours and adapting planning.

## Telling stories

### Context

This large two class Foundation 1 (F1) unit (with an intake of 55 children per year) has worked with a range of technologies to allow children to express and record their stories and ideas. Digital microphones, Talking Tins, Talk Time Cards and Digital Video are all used across a range of activities to enable children to build language skills and begin to develop appropriately sequenced stories. However, in the last year, the classes have begun developing the use of iPad minis to extend the range of scope of digital storytelling. The school purchased six iPad minis, which have begun to be used in a number of ways across the EYFS.

## Outline

One of the teaching assistants in this EYFS was very confident at accessing the iPad for personal use. Some of this experience included capturing still and video images with her family – from holidays, parties and other events. This experience enabled her to take a lead in using iPads for storytelling with the children. The initial focus was a simple approach using the video camera tools to allow children to investigate recording and viewing each other.

The school chose to use iPad minis and Griffin Survivor cases, which were slightly adapted to allow easier access to the camera. This allowed the children to be able to move freely around the EYFS, both inside and outside. At first, the staff just encouraged the children to record each other playing, taking part in activities and speaking to each other. After a short time, children were encouraged to make up stories – sometimes using props and toys that they could find in the EYFS. The iPad minis were then used to record the children telling their stories. Initially, one small group of children was particularly interested in creating and acting out stories. The children began to use the recordings to review their work and then they adapted and 'edited' the stories – re-recording them to see if they could make them better.

The EYFS had also bought an Apple TV, which was connected to a projector. The staff were able to share the children's work with their class groups. Children were encouraged to suggest how things be improved. Could different words be used? Could other props be used? Could other actions be used? This then began to encourage a much wider group of children to begin using the iPad minis to tell and record stories.

A storytelling project was being implemented across the school at the same time. The EYFS children had been visited by an external storyteller, who had worked with them to develop ideas for telling stories. These included story walk throughs, using props and developing expression. This input, alongside using the iPads, allowed the children to quickly develop structure, vocabulary and pace within their stories. The EYFS staff were particularly impressed by the way in which some children used the video to help them begin to write a written record of their stories, using pictures and early mark making.

After a few weeks of developing this project, the EYFS staff decided to review their progress. They took away the iPad minis for two weeks, reviewed the videos, looked at story records and then began to plan how they would like extend this further. After some discussion they decided that they would like to allow children to have discrete characters to move, manipulate and add voices. One of the EYFS teachers had recently seen the use of *PuppetPals* in a local school.

This app allows children to create animated films, using a range of characters, backgrounds and props. The app has a number of resources that can be used to quickly make short films – children are also able to record themselves adding dialogue or sound effects to the action that they create. Children can also decide whether to upload photos from the iPad camera roll to serve as characters or backgrounds for the films.

The EYFS teacher who introduced this app to the children talked candidly about how they allowed *PuppetPals* with live action films through use of the existing camera tools. The teacher created a task for children to investigate making both live action and *PuppetPals* films for the same story. The children were then encouraged to talk about how they felt the films differed and which they were happiest with.

## Early maths and phonics

### Context

This short case study describes the use of iPad apps to specifically develop early maths and phonics skills and understanding. Staff in the school decided to use iPads initially as a discrete tool to improve specific areas of knowledge. In this EYFS class (an F1 class of 25 children with a teacher and two TAs) they decided to develop the use of phonics and early maths apps.

### Outline

This EYFS class was given five iPads at the beginning of the academic year. Initially children were directed to investigate and explore a small range of creative apps for painting, music and drawing. The children were also encouraged to explore the use of the camera tools for still and video images. The class teacher then spent some time investigating apps that could develop early phonics and maths skills. As staff members were investigating the apps, the teacher developed an informal set of criteria which guided the choice of app. The areas included price, ability to reinforce teaching, quality/type of audio (the American accent was considered) and ability to work within the UK context (the use of US terms such as 'math').

The teacher initially downloaded a set of apps and tried these out with children in the class. This 'user' information was essential in discovering which apps actually easily impacted on learning. At the end of a few weeks the EYFS staff decided to provide a small set of apps for phonics, letter formation and maths. They chose a range of free, freemium and paid apps.

At first, these apps were provided on the iPads and combined with the use of other creative tools. Children were allowed time to explore iPad and app use and were encouraged to talk to each other and adults about what they were doing and learning. After a few weeks the class teacher decided to take a more focused approach to investigate whether directing children to use certain apps, following other types of teaching, could enhance and reinforce learning. Over a number of weeks small groups of children were chosen to have time on phonics or letter apps, immediately following small group phonics sessions. Other children were then directed to use the maths apps, following their own maths investigations and direct maths teaching.

The class teacher continued to observe and assess in the usual way – these notes provided some evidence of the impact of app use. Overall, the teacher felt that app use helped to consolidate and broaden the experiences that children were getting in other ways. In particular, the teacher felt that the phonics and letter formation apps helped to extend learning and give more opportunity to practice sounds and letters. Some children were much more engaged with the app environment and voluntarily spent more time working on these areas.

The class teacher also went on to speculate that the maths apps were able to help develop skills and understanding that could not develop in the same way without an iPad. For instance, the repetition and frequency of some skills, such as counting or coin sorting, was more dynamic and gave instant gratification and feedback. This encouraged some children to try out things that they would not normally explore – leading to greater confidence and time spent on these tasks.

# Discussion

Since 2012, there has been a steady and significant rise in the amount of tablet computers within English schools. BESA's (British Educational Suppliers) Tablets and Connectivity report (E-Learning Foundation, 2014) reveals that approximately one in five school computers are now tablets. This growth in tablet access has occurred in both primary and secondary sectors – however, more precise data about use in the EYFS is harder to find.

Young children's use of tablet computers (usually iPads) is frequently the subject of media scare stories. These stories highlight the perceived potential 'dangers' of using iPads, such as negative effects on motor skills or addiction (*Daily Mail*, 2014; *Daily Telegraph*, 2014a, 2014b). Certainly, articles of this nature can affect opinion about the use of tablets in schools for young children. The intention of this chapter was to provide practical and appropriate examples of the use of iPads – hopefully encouraging teachers to understand the potential benefits of the early use of tablets in the EYFS.

## Technology use and young children

There are an increasing number of diverse projects that research the iPad as a tool for learning. A number of these have a wide discussion focus looking at perceived benefits of using these technologies. Most studies focus on the impact in schools in general. For instance, Valstad (2010), in an early discussion of iPad use as a pedagogical tool, presents a focus on the multimedia learning benefits engendered by the design and functionality of the device. There are some examples of studies with an Early Years focus – for example, Kucirkova (2014) identifies three features of this tool which she feels will have a positive impact on early education:

> *iPads have three novel features which have the potential to make a positive difference to early education: iPads are portable and light-weight (unlike netbooks and laptops), they eliminate the need for separate input devices requiring certain levels of dexterity (such as mouse and keyboard) and thirdly, they are specifically designed to accommodate a number of apps, many of which have a child-friendly intuitive design.*

> (Kucirkova, 2014, p1)

Clark and Luckin (2013) speculate about how the iPad can add to the development of 'seamless' approaches to learning within classrooms, promoted by the tool's ability to develop interest, enagagement, independence, creativity and improved productivity. This chapter is similar to other discussions in identifying potential benefits of the appropriate use of iPads in classrooms. Fagan and Coutts (2014) present case study evidence of the impact of iPads on supporting collaborative learning, supporting creativity, inspiring learning and helping to develop documentation and assessment in early education. Other speculative discussions, such as McPhee *et al.* (2013), attempt to put forward reasons for what they describe as increased learner engagement, especially for boys. The ability to explore and structure information, as well as regular use of game based-learning features (such as extrinsic/intrinsic rewards, self pacing and goal orientation), are seen as major benefits for engagement allowed by iPad use.

Clark and Luckin (2013) continue their discussion by identifying specific instances of the benefits of certain iPad affordances, such as how portability enhances opportunities to promote greater face-to-face social interaction. This discussion compares other technologies, such as laptops or netbooks, and identifies how flexible and immediate ways of manipulating and structuring information in a variety of multimodal ways can promote sharing and learning.

A number of studies of technology use and young children centre on the nature of interaction and perceived impacts on thinking and dialogue. Stanton and Neale (2003) explore the potential of shared computer usage to generate collaboration, both in thinking and in dialogue. Suggestions from studies of this nature highlight how technological environments present ways of allowing shared approaches to achieve goals; pointing to the process by which computers can allow interaction that other environments may not allow in the same way. Wild (2011) identified the impact of shared use of computers on the thinking of dyads of 5- and 6-year-olds:

> *Nevertheless, it would seem that shared thinking could indeed be facilitated by planning for children to use the computer in a paired manner within the busy classroom to supplement the practice of a practitioner or teacher who may not always be immediately available to provide the kind of direct support of SST* [shared sustained thinking].

> (Wild, 2011, p230)

Specific discussion of the impact of iPads on thinking and dialogue is usually within the wider context of perceived benefits. However, there are a number of studies that have included discussion of the impact of the iPad interface on promoting learning and engagement.

Clark and Luckin (2013) suggest that learner motivation and engagement is promoted due to the immediate nature of the interface allowed by iPads. The touch-screen interface, whilst having certain restrictions such as restricted finger inputs, allows users to easily access and manipulate information, impacting quickly on learning.

Previous discussion of Kucirkova (2014) identities the lack of a need for separate input devices and peripherals – which require a certain level of dexterity – as having a major benefit, especially for young learners. Crescenzi *et al.* (2014) specifically study the nature of touch on the use of paper and iPad learning and painting activities. iPads as a tool – alongside other technologies such as paper, pencils and paints – allow a greater repertoire of touch-based communication skills. When discussing use of the iPad as a tool, the discussion suggests that *it engenders broader use of a wider range of types of touch, which include more complex and longer sequences of continuous touch interactions, fostering more elaborate touch repertoires* (Crescenzi *et al.*, 2014, p94).

## Barriers to tablet implementation in the EYFS

Tablet computers – and more specifically iPads – can have a range of issues that need to be considered before implementation in the EYFS. iPads are primarily designed for use in the home/leisure market. The nature of wireless access, access to files and personalisation are more suited for individual use rather than for working with groups or classes of children.

Clarke and Abbott (2013) also discuss some of the difficulties in letting young children access text using upper case 'keys' on screen keyboards; indeed, they call for Apple to take this into account in future iOS updates. However the case studies presented in this chapter perhaps show some practical approaches which may overcome access issues of this nature. Indeed text input and manipulation is perhaps not the greatest strength of iPad use – with other modes of communication enabled by intuitive software and embedded camera and microphone tools.

Some schools are cautious about introducing iPads into the EYFS, thinking that they could be easily damaged. Some of this reticence comes from a perception that young children could easily damage a technology that is so portable. McPhee *et al.* (2013) also suggest that schools' reticence can be due to entrenched views about the appropriate use of technology with young children – where the 'why aren't they talking to each other' or 'can't they play with sand and water' arguments dominate discussion and impact upon pedagogy.

The 'dangers' of technologies - 'real' or 'imagined' are captured within popular media discussion and coverage of this area. To some degree the need for a more widespread research-led understanding of potential pedagogical use could alleviate and mitigate this discussion.

## Future trends and potential

The research literature does not display any wide-ranging discussions of potential future trends and potential of the use of tablets and iPads in schools and early education. However an area that does receive some attention is the discussion of possible research trends. Kucirkova (2013) identifies the initial restrictions of early research focus. For example, a number of studies use an approach opposing digital vs non-digital ways of delivering education and learning. This approach often creates an 'unreal' restrictive focus on iPad/tablet potential by using oppositional discussion that does not represent the reality of classrooms, which can naturally combine both technological and non-technological pedagogical approaches.

Kucirkova (2013) also identifies the common discussion strand of technological determinism that seems to exist in some research approaches. A technologically determinist view maintains an approach that regards technology as the driver of change in society. A viewpoint of this nature pays less regard to the possibility that specific contexts and individual choices and approaches affect the impact of technology. Indeed

Kucirkova includes mention of a number of studies that regard technology as an educational 'panacea' for a range of problems and learning deficits:

> *There is a tendency to perceive technology, including iPads, as a quick-fix solution for outstanding educational problems, without giving due consideration to the idiosyncrasies of individual educational contexts.*

(Kucirkova, 2013, p2)

Research approaches are now accepting the complexities and potential of the innovative pedagogical use of iPads as tools within a range of learning contexts. Oppositional approaches lose any appreciation of exploring pedagogies and approaches that may not have been previously considered.

## App List for the Chapter

*2Simple 2Build a Profile*, *Evernote*, *PuppetPals* and *PuppetPals 2*.

A number of early reading, phonics and maths apps are included within the text.

## Further Reading

Burden, K, Hopkins, P, Male, T, Martin, S and Trala, C (2012) iPad Scotland Evaluation. Hull: University of Hull. Available from: **www2.hull.ac.uk/ifl/ipadresearchinschools.aspx** (accessed 20 December 2014).

A considered and developed discussion about the use of iPads within a range of different schools. This research report allows consideration of both the potential and existing impacts of iPads on teaching and learning in schools.

## References

Clark, W and Luckin, R (2013) *What the Research Says: iPads in the Classroom*. London: London Knowledge Lab, IoE.

Clarke, L and Abbott, L (2013) Hands on the iPAD, Heads in the Cloud: Teaching and learning with iPADs in a Belfast primary school, in McBride, R and Searson, M (eds) Proceedings of Society for Information Technology & Teacher Education International Conference 2013 (pp. 3672–80). Chesapeake, VA: AACE.

Crescenzi, L, Jewitt, C and Price, S (2014) The role of touch in preschool children's learning using iPad versus paper interaction. *Australian Journal of Language and Literacy*, 37(2).

E-Learning Foundation (2014) **www.elearningfoundation.com/Websites/elearningfoundation/ images/PDF%20Documents/Evidence/BESA_Report_Summary.pdf** (accessed 1 October 2014).

Fagan, T and Coutts, T (2012) *To iPad or not to iPad*. Available from: **www.core-ed.org/ thought-leadership/research/ipad-or-not-ipad** (accessed 27 October 2014).

Kucirkova, N (2014) iPads in early education: Separating assumptions and evidence. *Frontiers in Psychology*, 5: 715.

McPhee, I, Marks, L and Marks, D (2013) Examining the impact of the Apple 'iPad' on male and female classroom engagement in a primary school in Scotland. ICICTE 2013 Proceedings.

Stanton, D and Neale, HR (2003) The effects of multiple mice on children's talk and interaction. *Journal of Computer Assisted Learning*, 19: 229–38.

The *Daily Mail* (2014) **www.dailymail.co.uk/femail/article-2548365/As-revealed-one-three-children-use-tablet-talk-fathers-alarming-story-The-day-I-realised-toddler-addicted-iPad.html** (accessed 1 October 2014).

The *Daily Telegraph* (2014a) **www.telegraph.co.uk/education/educationnews/10767878/Infants-unable-to-use-toy-building-blocks-due-to-iPad-addiction.html?fb** (accessed 1 October 2014).

The *Daily Telegraph* (2014b) **www.telegraph.co.uk/technology/10008707/Toddlers-becoming-so-addicted-to-iPads-they-require-therapy.html?fb** (accessed 1 October 2014).

Valstad, H (2010) *iPad as a Pedagogical Device*. Oslo: Norwegian University of Science and Technology.

Wild, M (2011) Thinking together: Exploring aspects of shared thinking between young children during a computer-based literacy task. *International Journal of Early Years Education*, 19(3-4), 219–23.

# Chapter 6

# Technology outdoors

## Introduction

This chapter looks at the advantages of being able to use tablets to extend learning beyond traditional classroom spaces. We will consider how they can enhance outdoor learning by combining children's physical and digital exploration of the world, thinking about how outdoor scenarios can lead to active learning that is open-ended and child-led, and how tablets can capture these valuable experiences. By providing a context for talk and collaboration, technology can promote the development of communication skills alongside understanding of the environment, and enable children to make use of creative modes of communication. This approach is based on a constructivist view of learning, in which children interact with the world around them and with others to create their own frameworks of understanding, reflecting the ideas of theorists such as Vygotsky, Piaget and Bruner. We will suggest apps for making trails and treasure hunts using QR Codes, for manipulating media outdoors, and for using digital magnifiers and photo filters to record findings. And we will draw some conclusions about how the use of tablets beyond the confines of the classroom can help children take ownership over their own learning.

---

### Learning Objectives

At the end of this chapter you should be able to:

- identify a number of ways in which tablets could extend learning within an outdoor environment;
- plan the use of tablets outdoors to capture, share and present ideas in a range of media;
- suggest ways of differentiating children's learning with tablets outdoors;
- suggest ways of using tablets to help review and assess learning.

---

### Teachers' Standards

The following Teachers' Standards are particularly relevant to this chapter:

TS1 Establish a safe and stimulating environment for pupils.
Set goals that stretch and challenge pupils of all backgrounds, abilities and dispositions.

TS2 Demonstrate knowledge and understanding of how pupils learn and how this impacts on teaching.

Encourage pupils to take a responsible and conscientious attitude to their own work and study.

TS3 Promote a love of learning and children's intellectual curiosity.

Contribute to the design and provision of an engaging curriculum within the relevant subject area(s).

## Links to National Curriculum Programmes of Study

### Key Stage 1 and Key Stage 2

- Pupils become digitally literate – able to use, and express themselves and develop their ideas through information and communication technology – at a level suitable for the future workplace and as active participants in a digital world.
- All pupils are responsible, competent, confident and creative users of information and communication technology.
- Pupils should be taught to use technology purposefully to create, organise, store, manipulate and retrieve digital content.
- Pupils should be taught to select, use and combine a variety of software (including internet services) on a range of digital devices to design and create a range of programs, systems and content that accomplish given goals, including collecting, analysing, evaluating and presenting data and information.

# Example from practice

*Our Creative Village: using tablets to enhance outdoor learning*

**In the classroom**

## Context

This case study describes how technology supported outdoor learning through a half-termly, whole school project in our primary school entitled, 'Our Creative Village'. The project focused on ways of enhancing maths and English, focusing on the immediate environment around the school and the wider locality. One aim was to use our tablets to capture children's real-world exploration and allow us to bring their learning back inside the classroom for discussion and review. We hoped that this would make for a smoother, more connected learning journey that made sense to the children. We promoted the idea of children as explorers through the use of trails and treasure hunts, and emphasised the theme of discovery. An additional aim was to make the most of opportunities to combine physical and digital activity within the natural environment. Having achieved our initial focus on developing confidence and creativity in maths and English, we went on to consider how these approaches could be applied to science teaching.

Our class had been using iPads for two terms and had become confident in using a number of apps. Once their iPads were equipped with robust protective cases, the children were ready to extend their use of mobile learning to the outdoor environment. I will describe some examples of our English and maths activities from a number of year groups.

---

### Learning Objectives

Our intended learning outcomes were:

- to foster a sense of enjoyment and curiosity about maths and English;
- to encourage children to see maths as a creative discipline and a means for understanding the world;
- to help pupils develop confidence in using talk to develop clear thinking skills;
- to enhance writing skills through the production of multimedia;
- to use tablets to capture children's real-world exploration, and then review and extend learning in the classroom;
- To record and share our learning with the wider school community.

---

## Outline

### Outdoor maths

The theme for our outdoor maths was 'Trails'. One of our first lessons involved a digital scavenger hunt for Year 2 children in which they worked together to collect photos of real-world number arrays using the iPad camera. To give a few examples, they recorded rows and columns of parked cars and took close-ups of patterns on the cars themselves;

they came across five sets of five petals on a flower head; and they found regularity in configurations of leaves. Buildings were another source of evidence, with their arrangements of windows and solar panels. A walk further afield revealed number arrays in shop window displays, such as the symmetrical arrangement of fruit and vegetables. Children used the app *PicCollage* to pull the images they collected onto a single screen and annotated them with the relevant multiplication facts. Useful features of *PicCollage* are the ability to draw round and clip parts of photos, and to add text and arrows.

A similar activity in Year 1 focused on collecting examples of shapes in the environment and comparing their sizes using non-standard units. Once again, children were able to 'cut out' parts of photos with their fingers, arrange them on the screen and add words and arrows.

Further up the school, Year 6 children devised a Quick Response (QR) Code maths trail for Year 4 to complete. QR Codes are similar to bar codes. Text, videos or photos can be turned into a code using a QR Code generator and then decoded with a scanning app on a mobile device. The Year 6 children began by looking at the National Curriculum programmes of study for Year 4 and finding out what the Year 4s already knew. They aimed to make a set of practical and inventive challenges. Here are some examples:

- make a Roman numeral out of twigs;
- skip and count in multiples of six;
- how many triangles can you make with nine sticks?;
- find a natural object of an equivalent size to the gate;
- find a flower with an even number of petals;
- measure the angle of a pavement crack;
- illustrate a number pattern with natural objects;
- find the diameter of a tree;
- think of a method to count the number of bricks in a wall;
- design a playground game for learning a times table;
- make a tally chart for insects visiting a bush;
- make a Carroll diagram to sort stones.

Armed with their ideas, they used the free QR treasure hunt generator from *ClassTools*, (**www.classtools.net/QR**) to create text-based codes that did not rely on the internet. If the internet had been available outdoors, the codes could have been linked to uploaded images, sounds or videos. Another alternative is to use the site **www.qrstuff.com** to make codes that are colour-coded. This makes it easier to create differentiated activities and for several trails to take place at once. Our codes were printed onto photographic paper and placed around the outdoor environment using sticky Velcro. Finally, the Year 6 children made a talking avatar to introduce the activity using the app *Tellagami*.

**Figure 6.1**    A Tellagami avatar explaining the activity

It was then the turn of the Year 4s to follow the QR Code trail. They used the app *Scan* to decode instructions for each activity and recorded their solutions to the maths challenges using the cameras on their tablets. Some of their answers were recorded as short videos, some as photos, and some were just text or numbers. They assembled these as pages in the app *Shadow Puppet Edu* to make shareable multimedia presentations. The option to add voice-overs and text to each page provided an opportunity for them to tell the story of their experiences and reflect on the success of their strategies.

### Outdoor English

The theme for our outdoor English lessons was 'Points of View', and we aimed to use visual images to support written and spoken composition. Year 1 children began by photographing an outdoor object, such as an empty crisp packet, a tree, a car or a door. They planned a 30-second narration based on 'a day in the life' of their object, focusing on sequencing sentences and using time connectives. Using the app *ChatterPix*, they personalised their object by adding eyes and an animated mouth, and then recorded their spoken narratives. The talking animations were annotated with a sentence introducing the character and the finished talking images from each group were imported into *Shadow Puppet Edu*, where they were combined to make a slideshow with introductory music and explanatory text. These presentations were embedded onto the class blog so that they could be shared with a wider audience, and the children were delighted with the positive comments they received from friends and parents.

Year 2 children were given a selection of Lego figures and a brief to create Tiny People Tales using just six shots. They created and rehearsed their short stories through small world play outdoors and then took their photos. Some children chose to enhance their images by manipulating filters and colours in the app *BeFunky*. The photos were then imported into *My Story*, where children retold their fictional narratives through text and narration to make talking ebooks.

**Figure 6.2**  Six frame stories with Lego figures

Also working with the medium of story, Year 3 children explored settings, characters and plot in a theatre made from a natural outdoor space, using puppets made of natural materials. They captured their drama activities as images and short video clips, and then compiled them into *iMovie* trailers. *iMovie* trailers provide ready-made templates for dramatic short films in a range of genres, a simple technique that transformed our clips by adding transitions, text and music. If a trailer was too long, it was saved and re-imported as an *iMovie* project to allow access to the video editing options.

Children in Year 4 used drama to explore perspectives on the theme of positive values, thinking about the relationship between people and their environment. They used a freeze-frame technique to create three or four dramatic tableaux responding to prompts such as co-operation, hope, forgiveness, trust, friendship, freedom and tolerance. These were photographed and combined into a comic format using the app *Strip Designer*. Next, they filmed short 'talking heads' excerpts of dialogue. The app *ThingLink* was used to add interactive hotspots to the comic strips, which played their videos when touched. Back in the classroom the interactive comic strips prompted non-narrative writing on the theme of valuing the environment. Both the interactive comics and the pieces of writing were shared with the school community.

In Years 5 and 6, a number of photographic apps were used as a stimulus for thinking and writing. The app *RollWorld* enabled children to experiment with stereographic images that turn photos into 'miniplanets'. Manipulating the image using the sliders gave them many new perspectives on their environment and helped inspire creative writing.

**Figure 6.3** A stereographic image of a school playground using *RollWorld*

Some children chose to attach a small, light GoPro camera attached to their heads, a bike, a skateboard or a Wellington boot to capture action video shots. These shots were reflected and captured on the iPad in real time and pairs of observers created a commentary. Others used the iPad camera to make panoramic photos and went on to annotate these with interactive hotspots using *ThingLink*.

These unusual camera perspectives helped children to develop ideas around descriptions of settings, characters, atmosphere and dialogue. Back in the classroom, they used their images and films as prompts for narrative writing. They retold their stories standing in front of their visual media using the app *GreenScreen by DoInk*, together with a portable green screen, a stand and a clip. Alternative greenscreens included mid-green coloured fabric, backing paper, a painted wall or even a green *PowerPoint* slide on the interactive whiteboard. The result was a range of dramatic digital products uploaded to the class blogs, reflecting the children's desire to create an impact by combining exciting visuals with high quality writing.

# Taking it further

## Science outdoors

Having a received a good deal of positive feedback from parents, staff and children on our maths and English projects, we were keen to think about extending a mobile learning approach to science. An obvious application was to use the iPads as a lens through which to look more closely at the world around us from a scientific perspective via apps for magnification, slow motion and time lapse.

Our initial ideas included:

- record a rocket launch in slow motion;
- capture coloured ice melting;
- record the activity of bees around a lavender bush;
- make a time lapse video of the movement of clouds;
- collect close up images for a 'find the plant' quiz;
- annotate a photo of an organism.

Capturing these events would give us a stimulus around which to talk and think, and, most importantly, to make connections between ideas.

---

**Activity**

### Evaluating photography apps for science outdoors

Think about how the following apps could support scientific inquiry in the field by emphasising visual learning. Match each with a link to an aspect of the National Curriculum for science. Is there potential for some of these apps to be used in combination?

---

**Table 6.1** Apps supporting a visual approach to science outdoors

| App | What it does |
| --- | --- |
| SloPro | Makes slow motion videos |
| Miniatures: Tilt-shift time-lapse videos | Combines macro shots of scenes into time-lapse videos |
| ThingLink | Makes images interactive by adding links to other images, text or videos |
| Photosynth | Makes panoramas |
| Big Magnify | Zooms up to 8x to take close-ups |
| BeFunky Photo Editor | Creates photo effects and editing options |
| PicCollage | Combines photos into collages and clips |
| Trading Cards | Allows you to collect and categorise information as individual data cards combining words and images |
| Skitch | Annotates and labels photos |
| Brushes or ArtRage | Lets you draw and sketch, including over photos |
| Hyperlapse | Captures motion time-lapse videos and corrects for shake |

To put it simply, apps such as these offer new ways of looking at the world. We could see that visual approaches might inspire investigations in science just as much as the creative use of words in English. They could help us to discover and catalogue the natural world by photographing insects, condensing films of animal behaviour, exploring habitats, looking closely at colours in nature, or documenting our impact on the environment, to suggest a few examples.

Tablets can also help to record how outdoor science can be messy, physical and fun, as children explore the properties of materials such as ice, foam or water, make geysers, rockets, vehicles or parachutes, and investigate sounds and shadows. As teachers, we want children to make links between their memorable kinaesthetic experiences and the scientific understanding that underpins them. Technology can help us do this by capturing the noisy, physical experiences and then allowing us to calmly reflect afterwards, as we view the images or videos, so that the scientific concepts can be reinforced. A final stage is to turn the captured footage into digital artefacts that add text, annotations and narration to demonstrate and share understanding.

In addition to offering a visual approach to documenting scientific inquiry, tablets can support scientific fieldwork by making it easier to document, catalogue and record results. Rather than recording on paper, children can collect data to add to a collaborative spreadsheet. As they add new data, their charts will update. A single click can switch the results from a line graph to a pie chart and they can make decisions about the best way to present their results. The affordances of a selection of data handling apps are summarised below.

**Table 6.2**  Example apps for working with data

| App | Advantages |
|---|---|
| Numbers | Pre-made templates and styles for colourful graphs and charts |
| Google Sheets | Allows you to collaborate with others on spreadsheets |
| Google Forms | Automatically displays data as charts |
| iChart Maker | Gives you prompts to create a range of charts |
| Grafio | Turns your rough flow chart sketches into regular shapes and digital text |
| Haiku Deck | A slideshow app which includes a very simple chart tool |
| Teaching Graphs | Includes 'read' and 'make' options to develop understanding of a range of charts |
| Chart Maker | Displays a simple spreadsheet grid alongside the chart options |

# Discussion

## Learning approaches for using tablets outdoors

Our experience, then, suggests that there is considerable potential for using tablets in a cross-curricular way to enhance outdoor learning without compromising children's hands-on engagement and physical exploration of their environment. In this section we

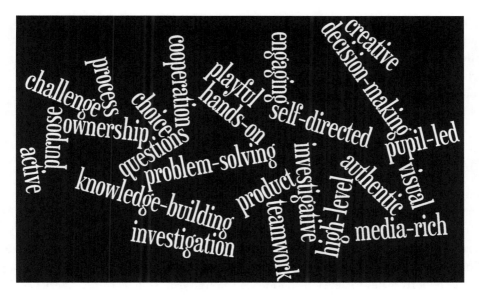

**Figure 6.4**   A word cloud illustrating some of the key words for technology supporting outdoor learning

will consider how this approach can influence learning and look at some relevant research evidence. The word cloud in Figure 6.4 illustrates some of the key emerging concepts.

## The development of mobile learning

Over the last five years tablets have become an accepted technology tool for learning and current trends suggest that their adoption is continuing (Traxler, 2010). A survey of over 550 US educators in May 2013 reported that more than 75 per cent of respondents have already adopted, or were very likely to adopt, mobile technology in the next one or two years (Interactive Educational Systems, 2012), and a recent *Horizon* report confirms that mobile computing is also increasing in UK schools (Clark and Luckin, 2013).

Several studies highlight the potential for tablets to offer unique learning benefits (Heinrich, 2012; Burden *et al.*, 2012). Many suggest that they can facilitate a high degree of personalisation in learning (Pegrum *et al.*, 2013), an increase in student independence (Alberta, 2012) and enhanced opportunities for collaboration (Henderson and Yeow, 2012). Researchers note that mobile learning can provide an effective bridge between indoor and outdoor learning and promote new forms of collaboration based on outdoor learning contexts (Pachler *et al.*, 2009; Clarke, 2012). Mobile learning is therefore opening up exciting opportunities for learning in a variety of indoor and outdoor settings, and its use is gaining momentum.

For example, a group of researchers at the Open University, led by Anne Jones, suggested six reasons why mobile learning might be motivating: Control, Ownership, Fun, Communication, Learning in context, and Continuity between contexts. They report that the association with informal learning outside school and the freedom to develop ownership over tasks increases intrinsic motivation: 'Feeling in control matters'

(Jones *et al.*, in Sharples, 2006, p16). A similar emphasis on self-directed learning emerged from a study completed at the University of Nottingham, which looked at children undertaking an outdoor treasure hunt activity. This team concluded that technology helped children to construct scientific meaning and provided a highly motivating and well-integrated context for their outdoor learning. They suggest that involving children in creating their own clues when making digital treasure hunts offers a way of maintaining motivation and enhancing reflection (Wyeth *et al.*, 2008, p31).

## The growth of outdoor learning

Within the wider context of outdoor learning, there has been a growth in Forest School pedagogy and in outdoor classrooms over the last 20 years, stemming from Scandinavian traditions that view closeness to nature as a natural aspect of children's learning. Our current EYFS framework requires settings to recognise the importance of daily outdoor activity. Part of the ethos of Forest School is to offer all learners regular opportunities to develop confidence through hands-on learning experiences that are responsive to needs and interests. Play and choice are integral features of this learner-centred approach, along with reflective practice (Knight, 2013).

In line with the ideas outlined above, we sought to unite physical and digital ways of looking at the world through our choice of activities, rather than replace one with the other. In our case study examples, children were immersed in the physical exploration of their environment. Tablets helped them plan, record and capture this, and to produce shareable digital products documenting the experiences. Sharing was important, as it encouraged children to build skills in synthesising and communicating ideas through various combinations of media. In this way, the technology reinforced the value of outdoor learning, as it was the medium through which clear links were made between indoor and outdoor activities, a requirement highlighted by Dillon *et al.* (2006) in their review of research on outdoor learning.

The value of using technology outdoors is borne out by a research study carried out by Acer and European Schoolnet in 2012, looking at the use of tablets in 63 schools from eight European countries. One of their recommendations is that teachers should exploit the use of tablets in learning contexts outside the classroom such as field work:

> *Evidence suggests that these type of practices, where tablets are used to extend learning beyond the formal classroom context, lead to more radical transformative changes in teaching and learning practices.*

> (Balanskat, 2013, p11)

## Choosing apps

In order to ensure that the physical and digital worlds are complementing and not competing with each other, we suggest caution in the number of apps you install. A common approach when starting to use tablets in schools is to focus on gathering a large collection of subject-specific apps. Rather than do this, it might be more useful to put together a core set of content creation apps that can be used time and time again across subjects. Once they gain confidence, children and their teachers will begin to be able to see ways in which to combine these familiar apps creatively to communicate and express their ideas. A core set of apps thus allows you to concentrate on embedding your devices into the learning process.

## Self-directed active learning

Focusing on a small number of open-ended apps for content creation can also help to make learning more pupil-centred and self-directed. It empowers children to take an active role in learning through constructing their own views and seeking evidence based on their engagement with the world. Although our children were all exploring the same outdoor environment, their responses were many and varied. Their confidence with the technology meant that they could record and share individual discoveries, making learning more personal. And their drive to find out and document was driven by the knowledge that they were working towards creating a professional-looking digital product.

The table below suggests some core apps to choose from for outdoor learning.

**Table 6.3**  A selection of core apps for outdoor learning

| App genre | Outdoor activity | Example apps and tools |
|---|---|---|
| Screencasting | Familiarising, recording, showing and explaining, synthesising understandings | *Explain Everything, Doodlecast Pro, PuppetPals* |
| Video | Filming outdoors, observing, roving reporters conducting interviews | *iMovie, Videolicious, Vintagio, SloPro* |
| Collages | Collating photos on a theme | *PicCollage, Moldiv* |
| Multimedia book making | Revising and sharing outdoor work | *Book Creator, My Story* |
| QR Codes | Trails and treasure hunts, scavenger hunts, geocaching, earthcaching, augmented reality | *Scan, QRStuff, QRafter, Huntzz, Aurasma, Geocaching, Spyglass* |
| Slideshows and media presentation | Reporting, documenting and sharing outdoor activities | *Shadow Puppet, Haiku Deck, Keynote* |
| Exploring sound | Sound walks, sound sampling | *SoundOscope, MadPad, AudioBoom, Croak.It!* |
| Posters and comics | Sequencing photos and presenting to an audience | *Phoster, Strip Design, Comic Life* |
| Diagrams and charts | Gathering data in the field, exchanging evidence, analysing and presenting results | *Numbers, Google Sheets, Google Forms, iChart Maker, Grafio, Chart Maker, Haiku Deck, Teaching Graphs* |
| Mindmaps and virtual walls | Concept mapping, posing questions, visual planning, collaborative note taking | *Popplet Lite, Bubble.us, Padlet* |
| Manipulating images | Observing, taking photos and editing or annotating them | *ThingLink, BeFunky, Big Magnify, Skitch* |
| Information organisers and quizzes | Cataloguing finds and discoveries | *Trading Cards, Quizlet* |

Many researchers draw attention to the fact that media-based approaches, such as we have described, allow for high levels of interaction and inquiry. They note that opportunities for pupils to engage in multimodal environments are expanding and suggest that learning can improve when children manipulate information (Fisher *et al.* 2013). Our children were active explorers and curators of information, taking pictures, recording audio and shooting video on location. Their use of apps transformed static words and images into artefacts they could investigate and explore.

This idea has resonance with socio-constructivist models of learning, which view children as co-constructors of knowledge through their interaction with people and the environment. Learning theorists such as Vygotsky, Bandura and Bruner, for example, recognise that learning is inherently social and that interaction is central to learning. As Llewellyn puts it, 'knowing is an active, adaptive, and evolutionary process' (Llewellyn, 2005, p28). In their definition of mobile learning, Sharples and his colleagues focus on the learning that takes place through interactions between learners and their surroundings as they filter new meaning about the world based on prior knowledge, and they suggest that technology can enhance this process:

> *The complexity of these interactions between learners, educational settings and mobile technologies challenges the conventional view of education as imparting knowledge in a fixed location, inviting a more expansive possibility of ubiquitous learning.*

(Sharples *et al.*, 2010, p2)

## The teacher's role in an inquiry-based approach

We have been thinking about how interactions between children and their environments can shape cognition, and how tablets can facilitate this. You will also need to give some thought to your own role. In order to help children to build on their prior knowledge you can help them engage with their initial understandings and preconceptions. This means encouraging children to pose many questions, and then taking a lead from their queries and allowing them choices in determining the direction of their projects. Such a process will help them to think about what they want to know, what they already know and what they need to know. As Hattie suggests, this may result in you talking less and listening more in order to achieve genuine dialogues and model deep communication skills (Hattie, 2012).

If you are to help children to understand and take control of their learning journeys, you will also need to demonstrate how you learn and make a deliberate attempt to make your own learning pathway visible:

> *Passion reflects the thrill, as well as the frustrations, of learning; it can be infectious, it can taught, it can be modelled, and it can be learnt. It requires more than content knowledge, acts of skilled teaching, or engaged students to make the difference (although these help). It requires a love of the content, an ethical caring stance deriving from the desire to instil in others a liking, or even love, of the discipline being*

*taught, and a demonstration that the teacher is not only teaching, but also learning (typically about the students' processes and outcomes of learning).*

(Hattie, 2012, p16)

A visible learning approach, as Hattie describes, continually models and monitors good learning strategies, gives relevant feedback and evaluates the impact of the teacher input and management of pace. When implementing these ideas outdoors with technology, you might consider how you can offer children multiple strategies, encourage risk taking and provide appropriate challenges. You could include learning intentions and success criteria that are highly differentiated for individuals. The aim is to give all children the chance to pose real questions and adopt an attitude of personal inquiry for their work outdoors. In short, we need to make sure to include time to *wonder* and time to *wander*.

It is likely that your outdoor experiences will be sandwiched between periods of time for preparation and reflection indoors. Within the classroom, as well, you will be able to use technology to help make the learning process more explicit. Think about using a virtual wall such as *Padlet* or a mindmapping app such as *Popplet* to gather ideas and to share reflections. An Apple TV can facilitate a review of work in progress by mirroring your iPads onto a larger screen. And the use of a pupil response app such as *Socrative* allows for quick polls at the beginning and end of sessions to check for prior learning and give peer feedback.

The diagram below illustrates how this type of learning can be an iterative process, in which inquiry, reflection and review are integral, and stages are repeated as children build upon them. Questions answered lead to new questions, and time is allowed for children to define and develop ownership of the problems or themes they intend to explore.

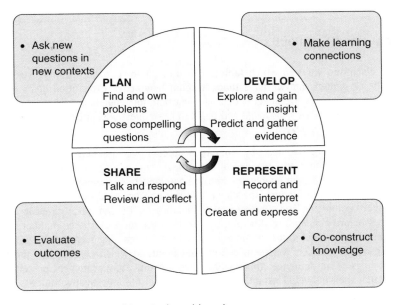

**Figure 6.5** The iterative process of inquiry-based learning

---

### Activity

Use the diagram above to analyse an outdoor learning experience with which you have been involved. Make your own version of the diagram and add some key words describing the physical activity and curriculum content. In a different colour, add some suggestions for ways in which tablets and apps could add value to the overall process.

---

## Accessibility and eSafety

One further consideration when choosing apps for outdoor activities is to think about the barriers that your children with special educational needs and disabilities (SEND) may face, and how particular apps and settings might help to address their accessibility issues. Some children will find it useful to use 'Speak Selection', voice recognition, or zoom and high contrast viewing options on iPads. For others, unfamiliar outdoor settings can be a source of anxiety, and previewing planned visits using photos and example scenarios can help build confidence. Concentration can be improved for many children through the Guided Access option within the iPad accessibility settings that restrict choices during an activity. Outdoor activities may need to be adapted to take account of certain children's physical needs and you might find an opportunity to give a child with mobility challenges increased responsibility for handling the tablets.

Thought also needs to be given to e-safety considerations and the appropriate use of sharing options when evaluating apps. The option within iPad 'Settings' to restrict certain websites and limit adult content can be useful, and you will need to evaluate the appropriate use of photographs when considering how best to share digital content.

---

### Summary and Key Points

We have discussed ways in which tablets can unite 'knowing' and 'doing' when working outside the classroom, and we have thought about how active exploration helps children to construct new meanings. We suggest that allowing time for reflection can help them to make connections with previous knowledge and begin to pose questions, applying their fresh understanding to different contexts.

The outdoor experiences we describe emphasise process over product. That is not to say that the product is not important; the use of technology can help to capture personal learning journeys outdoors, and then enable children to share and review them afterwards. By balancing the process and the product, the digital and the physical, and evaluating both, we make learning more connected and therefore more meaningful. We can quickly revisit and review experiences before moving forwards, and we can hold the reins of a large number of children as they pursue their own routes of inquiry. In this type of learning scenario the production of media-rich digital artefacts represent culmination points at which children can present their understandings to an audience. This collaborative pursuit of publication or presentation can draw together their individual strands of inquiry and fuel the investigative process by providing a huge injection of drive and motivation.

---

## Reflective Questions

How could you use questions to help children identify themes, issues and questions to explore in their outdoor learning, and how could technology help with this?

How could tablets help you to achieve a balance between children's direct experiences outdoors and the reflection and review needed to consolidate concepts?

How can you create learning goals that give a clear direction to outdoor learning with technology, whilst maintaining children's freedom to explore?

## Useful Links

The 'Our Creative Village' project described in this case study is loosely based on work undertaken at St Loys CofE Primary Academy, Weedon Lois in 2014.

www.st-loys.northants.sch.uk (accessed 20 December 2014).

Creative Star Learning

http://creativestarlearning.co.uk (accessed 20 December 2014).

A fabulous site full of practical ideas and information about learning outdoors and many examples of tablets used purposefully outside the classroom.

Pinterest Collection: Beyond the Classroom

www.pinterest.com/helencaldwel/beyond-the-classroom (accessed 20 December 2014).

A collection of over 100 links for using technology outdoors.

Uploads from The Slow Mo Guys

www.youtube.com/playlist?list=UUUK0HBIBWgM2c4vsPhkYY4w (accessed 20 December 2014).

A YouTube playlist focusing on capturing events in slow motion, many of which could be used to discuss science concepts.

Geocaching and Education

www.geocaching.com/education (accessed 20 December 2014).

An introduction to geocaching as an outdoor cross-curricular activity.

Technology Outdoors

http://mypad.northampton.ac.uk/ictoutdoors (accessed 20 December 2014).

Northamptonshire teachers sharing ideas for outdoor learning with technology in conjunction with the University of Northampton.

## App List for the Chapter

*PicCollage, Tellagami, Scan, Shadow Puppet Edu, Chatterpix, BeFunky Photo Editor, iMovie, Strip Designer, ThingLink, RollWorld, GreenScreen by DoInk, SloPro, Minatures: Tilt-Shift Time-Lapse Videos, Photosynth, Big*

*Magnify, Trading Cards, Skitch, Brushes, ArtRage, Numbers, Google Sheets, Google Forms, iChart Maker, Grafio, Haiku Deck, Teaching Graphs, Chart Maker, Explain Everything, Doodlecast Pro, PuppetPals, Videolicious, Vintagio, Moldiv, Book Creator, My Story, QR Stuff, QRafter, Huntzz, Aurasma, Geocaching, Spyglass, Keynote, SoundOscope, MadPad, Audioboo, Croak.it!, Poplet Lite, Bubble.us, Quizlet.*

## Further Reading

### What the research says: iPads in the classroom

Clark, W and Luckin, R (2013) What the research says: iPads in the Classroom. London Knowledge Lab [online]. Available from: **https://www.lkldev.ioe.ac.uk/lklinnovation/wp-content/ uploads/2013/01/2013-iPads-in-the-Classroom-v2.pdf** (accessed 18 January 2014).

A review of research literature related to teaching and learning with iPads in schools, including newspaper reports and blogs as well as academic papers, and consideration of the implications for different user groups.

### Active learning and teaching methods for Key Stages 1 and 2

**www.nicurriculum.org.uk/docs/key_stages_1_and_2/altm-ks12.pdf** (accessed 20 December 2014).

A booklet from Northern Ireland Curriculum giving a rationale and description of 79 active learning methodologies to integrate into learner-centred teaching.

### NMC Horizon Report 2014

**www.nmc.org/publications/2014-horizon-report-k12** (accessed 20 December 2014).

An annual report describing research findings from the ongoing NMC Horizon Project, which aims to identify and describe emerging technologies and key trends likely to have an impact on learning, teaching and creative inquiry in education.

### Introducing tablets in schools: The Acer-European Schoolnet tablet pilot

**http://1to1.eun.org/c/document_library/get_file?uuid=4507eca6-7707-4cfd-abe3-ad62b25ac847& groupId=10334** (accessed 20 December 2014).

A pilot study on the use of tablets to enhance teaching and learning practices across 63 schools in eight European countries.

## References

Alberta (2012) iPads: What are we learning? [online]. Available from: **http://education.alberta.ca/ admin/technology/research.aspx** (accessed 18 January 2014).

Balanskat, A (2013) Introducing tablets in schools: The Acer-European Schoolnet Tablet Pilot. Available from: **http://1to1.eun.org/c/document_library/get_file?uuid=4507eca6-7707-4cfd-abe3-ad62b25ac847&groupId=10334** (accessed 31 August 2014).

Burden, K, Hopkins, P, Male, T, Martin, S and Trala, C (2012) iPad Scotland Evaluation. Available from: **www2.hull.ac.uk/ifl/ipadresearchinschools.aspx** (accessed 18 January 2014).

Clark, W and Luckin, R (2013) What the research says: iPads in the classroom. London Knowledge Lab. Available from: **https://www.lkldev.ioe.ac.uk/lklinnovation/wp-content/uploads/2013/01/2013-iPads-in-the-Classroom-v2.pdf** (accessed 18 January 2014).

Clarke, B (2012) One-to-one tablets in secondary schools: An evaluation study. Available from: http://tabletsforschools.org.uk/wp-content/uploads/2012/12/2011-12-Final-Report.pdf (accessed 18 January 2014).

Dillon, J, Rickinson, M, Teamey, K, Morris, M, Choi, MY, Sanders, D and Benefield, P (2006) The value of outdoor learning: Evidence from research in the UK and elsewhere. *School Science Review*, 87(320), 107.

Hattie, J (2012) *Visible Learning for Teachers: Maximising Impact on Learning*. London: Routledge.

Heinrich, P (2012) The iPad as a tool for education. *NAACE and 9ine Consulting* [online]. Available from: www.naace.co.uk/publications/longfieldipadresearch (accessed 18 January 2014).

Henderson, S and Yeow, J (2012) iPads in Education: A case study of iPad adoption and use in a primary school. *In HICSS '12* Proceedings of the 2012 45th Hawaii International Conference on System Sciences, 78–87.

Interactive Educational Systems Design, Inc. (2012) National Survey on Mobile Technology for K-12 Education: Corporate edition. Available from: www.stemreports.com/products-page/market-research/2012-national-survey-on-mobiletechnology-for-k-12-education (accessed 18 January 2014).

Knight, S (2013) *Forest School and Outdoor Learning in the Early Years*. London: Sage.

Llewellyn, D (2005) *Teaching High School Science through Inquiry: A Case Study Approach*. Thousand Oaks, CA: Corwin Press.

Pachler, N, Cook, J and Bachmair, B (2010) Appropriation of mobile cultural resources for learning. *International Journal of Mobile and Blended Learning (IJMBL)*, 2(1), 1–21.

Pegrum, M, Howitt, C and Striepe, M (2013) Learning to take the tablet: How pre-service teachers use iPads to facilitate their learning. *Australasian Journal of Educational Technology*, 29(4).

Sharples, M (2006) *Big Issues in Mobile Learning*. Nottingham: University of Nottingham.

Sharples, M, Taylor, J and Vavoula, G (2010) A theory of learning for the mobile age, in *Medienbildung in neuen Kulturräumen* (87–99). VS Verlag für Sozialwissenschaften.

Traxler, J (2010) Will student devices deliver innovation, inclusion, and transformation? *Journal of the Research Center for Educational Technology*, 6(1), 3–15.

Wyeth, P, Smith, H, Ng, KH, Fitzpatrick, G, Luckin, R, Walker, K … and Benford, S (2008, April) Learning through treasure hunting: The role of mobile devices. In *Proceedings of the International Conference on Mobile Learning 2008* (pp27–34).

# Chapter 7

# Children as researchers

## Introduction

This chapter looks at how tablets can help children interact with the wider world by offering exciting ways of engaging in research and seeing themselves as information gatherers and creative producers.

As information becomes more of an integral part of our lives, from checking our friends' status on *Facebook* and sharing their links, to reading blog posts by fellow teachers on *Twitter* and catching up with the news online, the need to handle this information effectively grows. We will follow the journey of researchers as they begin choosing a topic of research to explore, become information gatherers and finally, creative producers to then use that information to communicate and collaborate with the world.

The following case study from Caroline Haslett School, Milton Keynes, shows a simple and effective way of implementing project-based learning in the primary classroom, utilising the tablet as one device that can source, organise and use information. It focuses on the varying stages within the research process and the questions which children must consider along the way, including how best to help pupils choose, evaluate and synthesise information with discrimination and how re-mixing and re-purposing information can reinforce understanding. A range of apps is explored to support gathering, organising and using information.

We will go on to discuss how project-based learning as a pedagogy for allowing children to be researchers facilitates the adoption of twenty-first-century skills. Part of this involves teaching children to become efficient and effective information gatherers and digital creators. Alongside this, we explore the informal learning culture associated with digital creation in online communities and how these practices can be utilised for education. The chapter ends by discussing the impact of children sharing their work with a global audience through simple video conferencing and eTwinning.

## Learning Objectives

At the end of this chapter you should be able to:

- recognise the range of twenty-first-century skills children need to be learning alongside the content curriculum;
- be aware of the benefits of project-based learning and how tablets can facilitate this;
- understand the process of effective searching, including relevant pedagogy;
- be aware of the range of digital creations children can create to share their learning.

## Links to Teachers' Standards

The following Teachers' Standards are particularly relevant to this chapter:

TS1 Establish a safe and stimulating environment for pupils.
Set goals that stretch and challenge pupils of all backgrounds, abilities and dispositions.
TS2 Demonstrate knowledge and understanding of how pupils learn and how this impacts on teaching.
Encourage pupils to take a responsible and conscientious attitude to their own work and study.
TS3 Have a secure knowledge of the relevant subject(s) and curriculum areas.
Foster and maintain pupils' interest in the subject.
TS4 Promote a love of learning and children's intellectual curiosity.
Contribute to the design and provision of an engaging curriculum within the relevant subject area(s).
TS5 Have a clear understanding of the needs of all pupils, including: those with special educational needs; those of high ability; those with English as an additional language; those with disabilities; and to be able to use and evaluate distinctive teaching approaches to engage and support them.
Demonstrate a critical understanding of developments in the subject and curriculum areas, and promote the value of scholarship.

## Links to National Curriculum Programmes of Study

### Key Stage 1 and Key Stage 2

- Pupils become digitally literate – able to use, and express themselves and develop their ideas through information and communication technology – at a level suitable for the future workplace and as active participants in a digital world.
- Pupils are responsible, competent, confident and creative users of information and communication technology.
- Pupils use technology purposefully to create, organise, store, manipulate and retrieve digital content.
- Pupils select, use and combine a variety of software (including internet services) on a range of digital devices to design and create a range of programs, systems and content that accomplish given goals, including collecting, analysing, evaluating and presenting data and information.

# Example from practice

*One year trial of 1:1 iPads in a Year 5 class at Caroline Haslett Primary School*

In the classroom

## Context

Year 5 at Caroline Haslett Primary School explored a geography-based project week (afternoons only) originally based around some lessons from the International Primary Curriculum's (IPC) 'What a Wonderful World' unit of work. Each day the team would be set a task that would allow children to independently pursue research topics, using many apps to make notes and collaborate. They created digital content to share their findings with the 'Board of Directors', in this case, their teachers, head teacher and a school governor.

---

### Learning Objectives

- to describe aspects of physical geography such as climate zones, biomes, rivers, mountains and volcanoes/earthquakes;
- to choose appropriate keywords for an internet search and use a range of ICT software and applications to create an end product suitable for purpose;
- to be aware of attribution, reliability, paraphrasing, copyright and Creative Commons when searching for information on the internet;
- to work collaboratively with peers to follow independent lines of inquiry.

---

## Outline

At the start of the week the children were randomly assigned into six groups and given access to a Dropbox folder (a folder containing any files you want that is shared with chosen people via the internet), so that the children could access any learning resources whenever they needed them.

*Stages of research in the digital age: from information gatherers to creative producers*   The focus of the week was on encouraging children to follow a process of information gathering and knowing how to find reliable information written at an appropriate level for them to understand. Figure 7.1 shows the flow chart I created to guide them through the research process.

As the children pass through these different stages, there is a range of apps suitable to support the development of each of these skills.

### Day 1

The first task was to find 12 calendar photos on the theme of 'Planet Earth' and include a caption explaining the choice. My lesson input discussed the law and ethics surrounding the use of images from the internet and included references to both

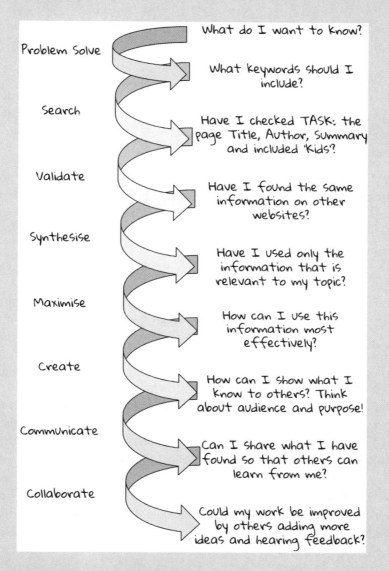

**Figure 7.1** Stages of research in the digital age

**Table 7.1** App suggestions for each research stage

| Search | Synthesise | Create | Communicate | Collaborate |
|---|---|---|---|---|
| Google Search | Mindomo | Haiku Deck/Flowboard | Edmodo | Google Drive |
| Encyclopedia Britannica | Notability | Google Drive: Slides | Tellagami | Edmodo |
| Dictionary.com | MindMash | Book Creator | Google Drive | Diigo |
| Google Earth | Notes | Halftone 2 | WordPress | Padlet (website) |
| Travel Atlas | Quip | Keynote | Dropbox | Nearpod |
| Safari | Skitch | TouchCast | Audioboo | |

copyright and Creative Commons. Now the groups were ready to start working their way through the flow chart!

## Problem solving and searching

The majority of the groups shared their ideas using a mindmapping app, such as *Mindomo*, to suggest possible themes and the individual photo ideas surrounding those themes. Following this, the groups shared their 'plan of action', uploaded it to a *Dropbox* folder and began searching for images.

When searching for Creative Commons images, the children generally used **www.compfight.com**, as this was a website we had used previously. One group remembered that the app *Haiku Deck* (an app for making presentations) searches Creative Commons images within it, as well as adding the reference on your behalf, and used that to directly import images into a presentation.

### Day 2

By this point, the children were expressing a wish to be able to communicate with their group. For this, I used the app *Edmodo*, which is an environment similar to a social networking site enabling group discussions, but with controls for teachers to ensure privacy and safety.

## Problem solving and searching

The task for day two was to research 'Biomes' and share what they found out. I suggested the children used the *Google Search* app rather than accessing the internet through a browser such as the *Safari* app. This was because they get less distracted with other websites. Here I emphasised 're-mixing' the information they found as opposed to copy and pasting; paraphrasing will become a useful skill in the future. My class favoured using apps such as *Mindomo* and *Notability* for their note taking, as these allow the use of a variety of different media such as photos, links, text and drawing. For those students who like clear organisation *Mindomo* is preferential as it is easier to see links between information.

### Create

As I did not specify what the children had to create, there were many different ideas suggested by group members. *Haiku Deck*, *Flowboard*, *Google Slides* and *Keynote* are more traditional presentation apps, although each offer different advantages. *Google Slides* allowed each child to work on their own iPad, whilst editing the same files. *Haiku Deck* and *Flowboard* were uploaded to a shared account via the internet, so that groups could work on their own sections and easily share their contributions. By contrast, *Halftone 2* is a comic-making app which offers an entirely different way to produce findings.

### Day 3

For the third lesson I wanted to show the class that information isn't just gathered from text-based sources. The main focus of the lesson involved using several pre-downloaded *Google Earth* maps (you can get some that use official NASA information, so it's well worth a look!) which allow you to cover the globe to illustrate a specific feature.

There are numerous advantages to using *Google Earth* instead of traditional atlases. First, the data shown here is accurate up to the time I downloaded the maps to share with my students. Most school atlases are at least 10 years old, and some even show countries that no longer exist! As well as this, you can layer several maps together, allowing the teacher to show both the rainfall this month and locations of the rainforest biomes.

Finally, the trouble with atlases is that they provide a 2D image, which means the countries have to be distorted in order to fit on the map and be clear. *Google Earth* eradicates this by presenting the world as a globe, accurately showing the scale and positioning of each of the countries. The only thing that children do need to be careful of is that they can flip the world upside down and not realise it if they try and navigate too quickly!

## Day 4
### Problem solving and searching
Each group explored different types of natural disasters, an activity which relied on using different sources of information gathering. For the 'factual' side of things I suggested that the children started with the *Encyclopedia Britannica*, as it gives some basic information which they can then build on with more specific search queries and searches on news websites such as **www.bbc.co.uk/newsround** and *Espresso*, as well as the *First News* newspaper app for live news stories aimed at 7–14-year-olds.

### Synthesising, maximising and creating
For this lesson the majority of the children used the *Notability* app, preferring the layout and style features to that of the *MindMash* app to collate their findings. We focused on 'maximising' and discussed the impact of the written word compared to other media. This led to the children suggesting that they could share their findings about natural disasters using video, as they believed that this would have the strongest impact. The majority of the class used the app *TouchCast* to make a 'greenscreen' news report or documentary using some green backing paper and still images they had found online, and placing themselves at the scene of their natural disaster. This lent a sense of immediacy to their work.

## Day 5
For the final lesson, I wanted to show the children how they could use the information that they had been gathering and processing over the last week. As a class, we participated in a 'mystery Skype'. This involves two classes Skyping and only the teachers knowing where the other class is situated. Each class has 20 questions to ask in order to try and guess the location of their partner class. Before we began, the groups formed their questions and then, in their teams, each child had a role such as using the *World Atlas* app to check for local rivers or *Google Earth* to check for recent rainfall.

## *Communicate and collaborate*

By communicating in this way, the children applied the research skills which they had learned to a real situation. After they had solved where the other class was located, the children shared the digital creations which they had made throughout the week using *Nearpod* to guide everyone through presentations in an interactive way and shared additional media through *Dropbox*. This gave the children in both classes a chance to learn from each other and share feedback.

# Taking it further

The examples of practice shared here are taken from a geography project week, but they could also be adapted for any subject, year group or key stage due to the open-ended nature of research-based projects. With younger children, I would give them a selection of pre-selected and age-appropriate websites, perhaps using an app like *Pearltrees* to make them easier to find, and then allow them to practise searching in a pre-defined context.

---

### Activity

Choose a line of inquiry that interests you; it could be to do with tablets and education or something completely different. Follow Figure 7.1 (Stages of research in the digital age) and complete each stage using apps you are interested in exploring. Aim to end with a digital creation that you can share with others.

Consider how you make choices throughout the inquiry. Which are simple choices and which are trickier?

Plan ways to teach specific skills for those aspects which you find more difficult to complete.

---

# Discussion

We will discuss the importance of these twenty-first-century skills as well as how using this project-based learning pedagogy nurtures children's development. Finally, we will consider the process of information gathering from the initial inquiry formation through to the digital creation, which children use to communicate their findings with a potentially global audience.

## Twenty-first-century skills

In twenty-first-century life, research skills are essential; from checking the news online, to finding out what apps to buy. We access information like this every day. From 2013–2020, the digital universe will grow by a factor of 10 – more than doubling every two years (EMC, 2014, p2). By 2020, September 2014's Foundation Stage children will be in Year 5, not even out of primary school yet.

This evolution of technologies has led to the introduction of the term 'twenty-first-century skills' and is recognised as necessary around the world (Ananiadou and Claro, 2009). These skills are most frequently described as being: collaboration, communication, ICT literacy and social/cultural competencies. However, most frameworks also mention creativity, critical thinking and problem solving (Voogt and Pareja, 2010). For example, collaboration today may mean working together without ever having met and communicating through video messaging (Dede, 2010), or it might involve ten teachers working on the same document, at the same time, to plan a scheme of work using the app *Google Drive*.

## Twenty-first-century teaching

The role of the teacher has changed from being the primary source of information (Kozma, 2003) to someone who facilitates, supports and scaffolds the learning process and aims to involve the teacher, peers and technology (Kim and Hannafin, 2011; Renner, 2006). Learning is a lifelong process, so our learners need to know where and how to find information (Siemens, 2005).

Giving children a range of sources of relevant, appropriately-levelled information sheets as well as a selection of pre-checked websites means that they view knowledge as something they receive from others (Dede, 2010), rather than seeing themselves as active curators and creators of knowledge (Renner, 2006). Resnick (2002) suggests that twenty-first-century learning should be project-based across subjects and that the role of the teacher is as consultant to their learners. This approach is frequently referred to as project-based learning and it encourages learners to become more active and take control of their own learning.

## Project-based learning

Project-based learning (PBL) involves children, often in groups, following a line of inquiry that interests them. This can be entirely open, or tied to a specific subject area depending on what you want the learners to focus on. During the geography case study above, I gave children quite a narrow channel for inquiry as this was something which they were not used to. From here, I then widened their opportunities and freedoms in later projects, so that they were not initially overwhelmed by the task.

Within PBL, the learners take responsibility for choosing their inquiry, brainstorming ideas and deciding how to present their project to show their findings (Bell, 2010). Tablets unify this process allowing the sourcing, publishing and sharing of content effectively and efficiently with one device (Renner, 2006). Introducing primary school children to these skills sets them up as lifelong learners in our very connected world.

Finally, PBL is a very inclusive approach for meeting individual needs. Although collaboration skills can be tricky, working in a group ensures that students can fulfil the roles suited to them. Whether they would prefer to be designing the presentation and organising the information, creating a timeline of key events from a non-fiction text or writing a diary of reflection, each child can display their learning as they wish. As well as this, the use of tablets means that children are not confined to desks and so can choose a learning environment best suited to their needs (Bell, 2010).

## Information gatherers

We are currently seeing a shift in focus of information and knowledge: it is no longer valuable, or viable, to be the 'knowledge holder'; with the digital universe growing by 1.7 megabytes a minute for every person on Earth (EMC, 2014) we would be fighting a losing battle if we retained this outlook. Instead, we need strategies for learning the things we don't know (Resnick, 2002) and we need to know where to find the information needed (Siemens, 2005). Unfortunately, this is not as simple as it might seem.

For children to become proficient information gatherers, their abilities need to include:

> *recognising that the 'safe' search filter can be turned on and off, an ability to formulate effective search strategies, interpret the results retrieved, judge relevancy of these results vis-à-vis given tasks, and possession of adequate reading skills.*

(Bilal, 2012, p1894)

## The process: searching, validating, synthesising and maximising!

### Searching

Once the children have decided on their line of enquiry, they must first choose a search engine. There are search engines designed specifically for children, such as Safe Search Kids (**www.safesearchkids.com**), KidRex (**www.kidrex.org**) and GoGooligans (**www.gogooligans.com**). Overall, children tend to prefer to use Google over more child-specific search engines, largely due to their familiarity with how it works (Jochmann-Mannak *et al.*, 2010).

There are other benefits to using Google: children often use 'natural' language when they search, for example, formulating questions like 'What food does a crocodile eat?', which other search engines find difficult to understand. In addition, Google's 'Did you mean?' feature helps them to correct spelling mistakes and the predictive dropdown that 'guesses' what you're trying to search for reduces the amount of typing required (Jochmann-Mannak *et al.*, 2010). Teaching children to use these shortcuts – as well as copy and paste – as part of the searching process can reduce the frustrations they experience (Foss *et al.*, 2013).

When teaching search techniques, it is important not to just give the children 'fact-finding' activities. Whilst these might prove a useful starting point, they are noticeably easier than a more open-ended research activity where the learner has to first consider the appropriate search query (Bilal, 2001). The deconstruction of the search query is one of the most difficult tasks for children to understand: often they can pick keywords but do not know where to go if this doesn't work. By combining search terms, and refining them based on results, children begin to see the search process as something that evolves rather than a 'one answer solves all' problem (Foss *et al.*, 2013).

Web-based search lessons, which focus on inquiry, offer children the opportunity to hone their skills in a real-life context (Kuiper *et al.*, 2005). In the real world, finding information is not the objective, it simply provides information that we can use to answer our problem and we want to replicate this in the classroom. In addition, finding the answer does not mean you have mastered searching; rather, you need to aim to find information in an effective and efficient way. Google offers a selection of lesson plans (including examples of progression), which you can access at **www.google.com/insidesearch/searcheducation**. There is also a 'Google A Day' (**www.agoogleaday.com**, accessed 20 December 2014) activity, which challenges participants to answer a research question using their searching skills (Foss *et al.*, 2013).

It is also important that children recognise that answers are not only found on websites, but also through 'how to' videos on video sharing sites such as *YouTube* (**www.youtube.com**). This is particularly important for those children who still rely heavily on visual cues when reading (Cooper, 2002) and for visual learners who are proficient readers. If access is an issue, you can always download a selection of these videos for your students to use, or encourage them to make their own.

Once the search query has been entered, several new skills need to be taught. First, children need to use reading skills, such as skimming and scanning text, to judge the success of their search – it may be useful to conduct this lesson as part of a guided reading session looking at real-world uses for these skills. Reading age is something very important to consider, as 13–16 year olds would still find some of the texts Google suggests challenging (Bilal, 2012). There are Reading Level filters built into Google's Advanced Search options which can help reduce the level of challenge: children should be taught to use these.

### Validating

When young children first see their search results, they tend to start clicking things in a prominent position and hoping to find what they need. This is one of the biggest ways in which children accidentally find adult content and advertisements, which causes frustration (Duarte Torres *et al.*, 2014). When you witness children doing this in the classroom, it is likely to be because they have not read and interpreted their search results. Boys frequently spend less time reading websites than girls (Large *et al.*, 2002) and so may be particularly thrown by this. Again, improving their skimming and scanning reading skills will help (Bilal and Kirby, 2002).

Assessing the relevance of the search engine results is an area that children struggle with (Bilal, 2012). In the classroom, I tend to use the acronym TASK (Title, Author,

**Figure 7.2**  TASK to check the validity of suggested pages

Summary, Kids) to encourage children to think about the reliability and validity of links they are presented with.

First children must look at the title and check that it matches their search. Next, they check the 'author' or 'address' and consider if it's a good source. An important learning exercise can be to discuss sources and talk about different web suffixes such as .org, .com etc., as well as the difference between websites, blogs and wikis. Exposing children to a pool of reliable sources and explaining why they are reliable makes it more likely that they will make informed choices when searching independently (Foss *et al.*, 2013). They can also be encouraged to look in the summary for more information about whether the site is the one they are searching for.

Finally, children should check if they can find the same information on several web pages. This ensures that fake websites (such as the 'Tree Octopus' **http://zapatopi.net/ treeoctopus**, accessed 20 December 2014) are soon foiled.

### Synthesising and maximising

Before children can become digital creators, they must first make use of the information that they have gathered. This involves using evaluating and interpreting skills in order to build knowledge (Bilal and Kirby, 2002; Bilal, 2012; Walraven *et al.*, 2008). Here, the children are reflecting on how they can make the best use of the information. It is important that this stage is not omitted, as it is where a lot of the content-based learning happens.

## Creative producers

Here are some interesting facts: every 60 seconds in 2014, 67,000 photos are uploaded to *Instagram* and 360,000 minutes of video are uploaded to *YouTube*. As well as this, 50,000 links are shared on *Facebook*, 1800 new *WordPress* blog posts are written and 4.7 million *Tumblr* posts are blogged and reblogged (Qmee, 2014). The year 2014 is full of creative producers and the process has become so natural that many people do not even realise they are doing it.

Furthermore, *Instagram*, *WordPress*, *Tumblr*, *Blogger* and *YouTube* all featured in the top 50 web entries accessed by children aged 6–14 in the UK. Each year there is a rise in 8–11 year olds using websites such as *Flickr*, *Instagram* and *Snapfish*, as well as those using their phone to put photos or videos on sites like *YouTube*, *Facebook* or *Instagram* (Ofcom, 2013). This does not include other online communities that children may participate in, such as *Scratch*, which has approximately 940,000 registered users, aged between 4 and 11 (Scratch, 2014).

## The process: creating, communicating and collaborating

### Creating

Bloom's revised taxonomy placed 'creating' as the highest order thinking skill (Anderson and Krathwohl, 2000) and suggested this would show true mastery and understanding of a topic. This is where teaching with tablets really shines, as technology is such a creative tool. Resnick (2002) suggests that we should think of technology as more like finger paint than television. Televisions only deliver information, whereas finger paint allows you to design and create things. In line with the digital age, Churches (2008) has since amended Bloom's revised taxonomy, calling it 'Bloom's digital taxonomy'. Figure 7.3 combines each of the stages with their modern skills verbs.

Higher-Order Thinking Skills

| | |
|---|---|
| Creating | Programming, filming, animating, blogging, video blogging, mixing, remixing, wiki-ing, publishing, videocasting, podcasting, directing/producing, creating or building mash ups. |
| Evaluating | (Blog/vlog) commenting, reviewing, posting, moderating, collaborating, networking, reflecting, (alpha & beta) testing |
| Analysing | Attributing, outlining, finding, structuring, integrating, mashing, linking, reverse-engineering, cracking, mind-mapping, validating, tagging |
| Applying | playing, operating, hacking, uploading, sharing, editing |
| Understanding | Advanced searching, boolean searching, blog journaling, twittering, categorising and tagging, commenting, annotating, subscribing |
| Remembering | Bullet pointing, highlighting, bookmarking, social networking, social bookmarking, favorite-ing/local bookmarking, searching, googling |

Lower-Order Thinking Skills

**Figure 7.3** Churches' (2008) Bloom's digital taxonomy list of skills

As you can see, technology offers the most variety of opportunities during the 'create' stage of this taxonomy. The list of opportunities for allowing children to be creative producers in your classroom is endless. However, it is important to remember that asking children to make a podcast about the Romans does not mean that by the end of the activity they will indeed understand what they needed to know about the Romans. Technology is merely the mediator that presents the content the children have already learned and understood. To this end, we need to ensure that we have first considered the content that we are covering as well as the pedagogy we are using to communicate with our learners. From here, we can then match the technology tools to our learner's needs (Bower *et al.*, 2010).

When teaching using these new technologies, particularly web-based applications, it is important to discuss e-safety. For example, before you use an app you should know what happens to your content – does it save online? Can you control who sees it? Not only this, but, as children are learning new roles, they also need a basic understanding of copyright such as not taking images without attribution and using paraphrasing when using internet-based sources, as well as plagiarism and the difference between re-mixing and stealing ideas.

Re-mixing and re-using content via social websites is a growing practice. An example is the *Scratch* website for sharing re-usable computing projects. The idea of taking someone else's work and changing or adding to it can be difficult for children, who think of someone else using their ideas as 'copying'. Younger users of *Scratch* are more likely to complain about plagiarism than older users. This may be because they have less understanding about what re-mixing is and its potential benefits (Hill *et al.*, 2010). They may also feel that human-written credit should be given for their work in order to distinguish re-mixing from theft (Monroy-Hernández *et al.*, 2011). Understanding the benefits of working in an open-source way and sharing ideas could benefit classroom culture as well. Think about when you share ideas in writing, or discuss how you solved a problem in maths.

Creative producing often coincides with an online community. These groups often have what Jenkins (2006) refers to as a 'participatory culture', which simply means an environment where creativity is actively encouraged and shared with the group. Within these informal learning environments, there are often also social connections and an acceptance of any contributions submitted. Jenkins goes on to suggest that these communities offer opportunities for peer learning, the development of useful skills, changes in attitudes towards sharing ideas and empowered citizenship. Creating such a culture within a classroom could have huge potential. Ito *et al.* (2008) stress that the characteristics of peer-based learning in these communities are based around reciprocity and the idea that peers, of equal authority, can produce and evaluate together.

### Communicating and collaborating

We have already discussed the use of online communities as a way of empowering children to share their creations as well as collaborating to work together to create even better projects (Renner, 2006). If you cannot use existing online communities, or there aren't any that suit your purpose, blogs and wikis are a great way of creating a community, allowing children to share their learning experiences with a real-world audience. Many children and young people already use blogs as a way of reflecting on their social lives or their individual interests, and with careful prompting this can be turned into a powerful metacognitive tool for outwardly reflecting on learning (Crook, 2008).

Finally, communicating and collaborating can be taken to the next step through digital projects such as *Skype in the Classroom* (**https://education.skype.com**) and *E-Twinning* (**www.etwinning.net**, accessed 20 December 2014), which are websites that allow teachers to meet and engage collaboratively on projects of shared interests with the class. Projects can range from a one-off *Skype* call, to a continual *Edmodo* discussion about a topic or a shared wiki or blog which is added to regularly by both classes. The internet allows for simple collaboration between students in neighbouring classrooms, on different sides of a town or on the other side of the planet (Fryer, 2014). We should be making the most of this.

To finish, technology is an integral part of children's lives and, as digital natives, they do not think twice about using these resources. As educators, we have an important role in ensuring that learners know how to do this safely, as well as shaping that use into something that is beneficial to learning:

> *If we do not work with social media and associated literacies, not only do we deprive students of considerable educational benefits, but we will find that, for students, literacies acquired outside of the classroom will come to seem more relevant that those acquired within it.*

(Pegrum, 2011, p29)

---

## Activity

Spend some time looking at Figure 7.3 Churches' (2008) Bloom's digital taxonomy list of skills.

Choose three digital skills that are new to you and spend some time researching and practising them. You might like to look for examples and then create your own, which you could use as a model when you introduce it to your class.

---

## Summary and Key Points

We have looked at how tablets can facilitate children as researchers in the classroom, through simple access to the internet and the use of a sole device to explore, collect and analyse information before using it to create a range of digital artefacts. As well as this, we considered the pedagogical advantages of teaching through project-based learning and using this as a means to address, and teach, twenty-first-century skills such as problem solving, communication and collaboration.

The 'stages of research in the digital age' flow chart suggested in this chapter focuses both the teacher and the learners on the numerous steps involved in being a researcher. Different amounts of time will need to be spent on each aspect, but, by following through each stage, children will develop a deeper understanding of the topic studied. Particular attention should be paid to the 'communicating' and 'collaborating' aspects, as the use of the internet to provide an authentic, global audience can never be over-estimated.

We focused our discussion on the challenges faced by children as internet researchers and how best to prepare them for life in a workplace where this is likely to be an everyday occurrence. Directly teaching twenty-first-century skills, and encouraging children to reflect on their progress at developing them, is one way forward. As well as this, we considered the best strategies to teach learners to ensure effective and efficient searching and discussed the range of digital creations made possible by the use of tablets.

Remember, when using the internet, even with filters, it is important that children understand what they should do if they find information they are uncomfortable with. As well as this, teaching research skills provides a great opportunity to discuss appropriate sources, the difference between fact and opinion and the validity of sources. Other ICT issues can also be explored such as copyright, Creative Commons, plagiarism, attribution and re-mixing.

---

## Useful Links

- https://education.skype.com (accessed 20 December 2014)

- www.etwinning.net (accessed 20 December 2014)

- www.google.co.uk/insidesearch/searcheducation/lessons.html (accessed 20 December 2014)

- www.swaygrantham.co.uk (accessed 20 December 2014)

- http://ictmagic.wikispaces.com/ICT+%26+Web+Tools (accessed 20 December 2014)

## App List for the Chapter

iPad apps: *Google Search, Encyclopedia Britannica, Dictionary.com, Google Earth, Travel Atlas, Safari, Mindomo, Haiku Deck, Flowboard, Edmodo, Google Drive, Notability, Tellagami, MindMash, Book Creator, Diigo, Notes, Halftone 2, WordPress, Quip, Keynote, Dropbox, Nearpod, Skitch, TouchCast, Audioboo, Skype, First News Newspaper*

Android apps: *Google Search, Encyclopedia Britannica, Dictionary.com, Google Earth, Safari, Mindomo, Edmodo, Google Drive, Tallagami, Book Creator, Notes, Diigo, WordPress, Quip, DropBox, Nearpod, Skitch, Audioboo, Skype*

Windows apps: *Google Search, Encyclopedia Britannica, Edmodo, Notes, DropBox, Nearpod, Skitch, Audioboo, Skype*

Web-based tools: *Google Search, Encyclopedia Britannica, Dictionary.com, Google Earth, Mindomo, Haiku Deck, Flowboard, Edmodo, Google Drive, WordPress, Quip, Dropbox, Nearpod, Audioboo, Skype*

## Further Reading

Bell, S (2010) Project-based learning for the 21st century: Skills for the future. *The Clearing House*, 83(2), 39–43.

A clear explanation of what PBL is and more detail about how to develop it in the classroom.

www.skills21.org (accessed 20 December 2014)

American website with discussion of their beliefs about 21st-century skills.

Creative Commons 101: An introduction to CC licences. Available from: www.wired.co.uk/news/archive/2011-12/13/creative-commons-101 (accessed 20 December 2014)

An article discussing Creative Commons, copyright and licensing.

## References

Ananiadou, K and Claro, M (2009) 21st Century Skills and competences for New Millennium learners in OECD countries. Organization for Economic Cooperation and Development. EDU Working paper no. 41.

Anderson, LW and Krathwohl, DR (2000) *A Taxonomy for Learning, Teaching, and Assessing: A Revision of Bloom's Taxonomy of Educational Objectives*. Boston, MA: Allyn & Bacon.

Bell, S (2010) Project-based learning for the 21st century: Skills for the future. *The Clearing House*, 83(2), 39–43.

Bilal, D (2001) Children's use of the Yahooligans! Web search engine: II. Cognitive and physical behaviors on research tasks. *Journal of the American Society for Information Science and Technology*, 52(2), 118–36.

Bilal, D (2012) Ranking, relevance judgment, and precision of information retrieval on children's queries: Evaluation of Google, Yahoo!, Bing, Yahoo! Kids, and ask Kids. *Journal of the American Society for Information Science and Technology*, 63(9), 1879–96.

Bilal, D and Kirby, J (2002) Differences and similarities in information seeking: Children and adults as Web users. *Information Processing & Management*, 38(5), 649–70.

Bower, M, Hedberg, JG and Kuswara, A (2010) A framework for Web 2.0 learning design. *Educational Media International*, 47(3), 177–98.

Churches, A (2008) Bloom's taxonomy blooms digitally. Tech & Learning, 1. Available from: **http://edorigami.wikispaces.com/file/view/bloom%27s%20Digital%20taxonomy%20v3.01. pdf/65720266/bloom%27s%20Digital%20taxonomy%20v3.01.pdf** (accessed 2 September 2014).

Crook, C (2008) Web 2.0 technologies for learning: The current landscape – opportunities, challenges and tensions. BECTA Research Report. Available from: http://dera.ioe.ac.uk/1474/1/becta_2008_web2_ currentlandscape_litrev.pdf (accessed 2 September 2014).

Dede, C (2010) Comparing frameworks for 21st century skills, in Bellanca, J and Brandt, R (eds) *21st Century Skills: Rethinking How Students Learn*. Bloomington, IN: Solution Tree Press, pp51–76.

Duarte Torres, S, Weber, I and Hiemstra, D (2014) Analysis of search and browsing behavior of young users on the web. *ACM Transactions on the Web* (TWEB), 8(2).

EMC (2014) The digital universe of opportunities: Rich data and the increasing value of the internet of things. Available from: **www.emc.com/leadership/digital-universe** (accessed 25 August 2014).

Foss, E, Druin, A, Yip, J, Ford, W, Golub, E and Hutchinson, H (2013) Adolescent search roles. *Journal of the American Society for Information Science and Technology*, 64(1), 173–89.

Fryer, WA (2014) Skype in the classroom. *Publications Archive of Wesley Fryer*, 1(1).

Hill, BM, Monroy-Hernández, A and Olson, KR (2010, May) Responses to remixing on a social media sharing website. In *Proceedings of the AAAI International Conference on Weblogs and Social Media (ICWSM '10)*.

Ito, M, Horst, H, Bittanti, M, Boyd, D, Herr-Stephenson, B, Lange, PG, Pascoe, CJ and Robinson, L (2008) *Living and Learning with New Media: Summary of Findings from the Digital Youth Project*. John D. and Catherine T. MacArthur Foundation.

Jenkins, H (2006) *Confronting the Challenges of Participatory Culture: Media Education for the 21st Century. An Occasional Paper on Digital Media and Learning*. John D. and Catherine T. MacArthur Foundation.

Jochmann-Mannak, H, Huibers, T, Lentz, L and Sanders, T (2010) Children searching information on the internet: Performance on children's interfaces compared to Google, in *Workshop on Accessible Search Systems, SIGIR 2010*, Geneva, Switzerland, 27–35.

Kim, MC and Hannafin, MJ (2011) Scaffolding problem solving in technology-enhanced learning environments (TELEs): Bridging research and theory with practice. *Computers & Education*, 56(2), 403–17.

Kozma, RB (2003) Technology and classroom practices: An international study. *Journal of Research on Technology in Education*, 36(1), 1–14.

Kuiper, E, Volman, M and Terwel, J (2005) The Web as an information resource in K–12 education: Strategies for supporting students in searching and processing information. *Review of Educational Research*, 75(3), 285–328.

Large, A, Beheshti, J and Rahman, T (2002) Gender differences in collaborative web searching behavior: An elementary school study. *Information Processing & Management*, 38(3), 427–43.

Ofcom (2013) Children and parents: Media use and attitudes report. Available from: **http://stakeholders. ofcom.org.uk/binaries/research/media-literacy/october-2013/research07Oct2013.pdf** (accessed 20 August 2014).

Pegrum, M (2011) Modified, multiplied and (re)mixed: Social media and digital literacies, in Thomas, M (ed.) *Digital Education: Opportunities for Social Collaboration*. Basingstoke: Palgrave MacMillan, pp9–36.

Qmee (2014) Online in 60 seconds: A year later [Infographic]. Available from: **http://blog.qmee.com/ online-in-60-seconds-infographic-a-year-later** (accessed 20 August 2014).

Renner, W (2006) *E-learning 2.0: New frontier for student empowerment*. Sydney: The University of Sydney, Australia.

Resnick, M (2002) Rethinking learning in the digital age, in Kirkman, G, Cornelius, P, Sachs, J and Schwab, K (eds) *The Global Information Technology Report 2001–2002*. New York: Oxford, 4.

Scratch (2014) Community statistics at a glance. Available from: **http://scratch.mit.edu/statistics** (accessed 2 September 2014).

Siemens, G (2005) Connectivism: A learning theory for the digital age. *International Journal of Instructional Technology and Distance Learning*, 2(1), 3–10.

Voogt, J and Pareja Roblin, N (2010) *21st Century Skills*. University of Twente, Enschede.

Walraven, A, Brand-Gruwel, S and Boshuizen, H (2008) Information-problem solving: A review of problems students encounter and instructional solutions. *Computers in Human Behavior*, 24(3), 623–48.

# Chapter 8

# Computing

## Introduction

This chapter discusses the relevant pedagogical approaches and assessment opportunities when teaching computer science with tablets, and illustrates these with case studies from a primary classroom. We then look at activity ideas across year groups linked to the National Curriculum programmes of study and provide useful resources that will support teachers to further their knowledge and understanding in this area.

Mobile devices provide many opportunities for teaching computer science concepts, from problem-solving activities using puzzle-like apps to writing programs to achieve specific goals using visual programming apps. Learning computational logic on tablets that can be carried around means instant gratification for students, as they can share their programs with their friends, check for errors, and receive immediate feedback on their work. We will look at apps that will help students to understand computer science terminologies and concepts such as 'algorithm', 'procedures', 'variable', 'sequences', 'loops', 'decomposition' and 'conditionals', and we will suggest the use of 'unplugged' activities away from the computer where appropriate. Additionally, we will explore children's problem-solving activities on tablets as a context for them to actively construct knowledge through experiment and discovery. Based on a constructionist learning approach, this constant and continual 'problem-solving' process also enables children to develop knowledge about their learning as they exercise the planning, decision-making, organising, testing and evaluating skills that are fundamental to metacognitive awareness (Fisher, 2005; Schraw *et al.*, 2006; Sternberg, 1998). Alongside this, we are aware that selecting suitable apps and designing appropriate activities to support learners to develop specific skills, and achieve desired learning outcomes, is a vital but a difficult task. We will therefore share activity ideas for some of the apps we discuss, to be used across the year groups, with examples.

---

### Learning Objectives

At the end of this chapter you should:

- be able to describe some key terms of computer science and the concepts required to teach the computing curriculum;
- have some knowledge of computational thinking and how to apply computational thinking approaches to solve problems using tablets;

---

- be aware of a number of pedagogical approaches to teaching and learning programming concepts using apps on tablets;
- be able to design activities to teach the computer science element of the computing curriculum using appropriate apps on tablets.

## Links to Teachers' Standards

The following Teachers' Standards are particularly relevant to this chapter:

TS1 Establish a safe and stimulating environment for pupils.
Set goals that stretch and challenge pupils of all backgrounds, abilities and dispositions.
TS2 Guide pupils to reflect on the progress they have made and their emerging needs.
Demonstrate knowledge and understanding of how pupils learn and how this impacts on teaching.
Encourage pupils to take a responsible and conscientious attitude to their own work and study.
TS3 Promote a love of learning and children's intellectual curiosity.
Contribute to the design and provision of an engaging curriculum within the relevant subject area(s).

## Links to National Curriculum Programmes of Study

This chapter is relevant to the new Primary Computing Curriculum in England for Key stages 1 and 2, which defines computer science as the core element of computing (DfE, 2013). The following strands in Key Stage 1 and Key Stage 2 subject content will be covered in this chapter.

### Key Stage 1

- understand what algorithms are; how they are implemented as programs on digital devices; and that programs execute by following precise and unambiguous instructions;
- create and debug simple programs;
- use logical reasoning to predict the behaviour of simple programs.

### Key Stage 2

- design, write and debug programs that accomplish specific goals, including controlling or simulating physical systems; solve problems by decomposing them into smaller parts;
- use sequence, selection, and repetition in programs; work with variables and various forms of input and output;
- use logical reasoning to explain how some simple algorithms work and to detect and correct errors in algorithms and programs.

# Example from practice

*Creating a racing game using the Hopscotch app*

**In the classroom**

## Context

This case study reports on a four-part lesson as part of the computing curriculum in a Year 5 class during a spring term, in which children were asked to create a 'racing game' using the *Hopscotch* app on iPads. The aim of the lesson was to provide a context for children to design and write programs that include sequencing, repetition, procedures and variables. The children had previously used the *Scratch* program for creating simple games, so they were aware that computers do what they are told, and in the order they are told. These lessons provided them with an opportunity to apply and develop their step-by-step thinking skills in a different programming environment. Children were allowed to work in pairs, in groups or individually, however no one chose to work alone. They first drew their game design on paper and annotated it to define the procedures that they needed to write. They constantly checked their programs for errors and corrected them, either independently or with the support of a friend. Having a mobile device that can be carried around as a learning tool made it much easier to move around and look at what others were doing or ask for help. Children reflected on their programs through discussions with their partners and the whole class, both during the activity and at the end of the sessions.

---

### Learning Objectives

Intended learning outcomes for these four sessions were:

- to design and write simple programs to achieve a specific outcome;
- to identify errors and solve problems by decomposing them into smaller parts;
- to use sequence, selection and repetition in programs;
- to work with variables and different forms of input/output in programs.

---

## Outline

### Getting to know the Hopscotch app

*Hopscotch* is an iPad app that provides a drag-and-drop programming environment. Using *Hopscotch* you can create drawings, mathematical shapes, simple interactive games and animated stories. You select characters and then use rules to tell the object what to do. Each rule has an event (e.g. 'when project started') and an ability, which is a sequence of tasks for the object to complete (e.g. 'go left', 'wiggle'). Once you have selected the rule, you can drag blocks from the menu on the left-hand side to the middle to create a script. The *Hopscotch* app comes with many built-in characters and it is also possible to use the Emoji keyboard with iPads, which provides many more characters and objects for your project.

## Lesson sequence

- In the first session we explained to children that they would be creating a racing game using the *Hopscotch* app. We started by discussing what they already knew about designing and making games, and about using different programs on computers and tablets. This enabled us to differentiate the tasks for learners with different needs. We asked them to list any words that they knew or remembered about making games and wrote them on the display board on a wall. They were told that they could add any new vocabulary that they learned during the sessions to the list

- Unplugged! Next we took the children to the school hall, where we designed a racing track with obstacles using tissue paper. Two children acted as racing cars and the rest of the class gave instructions to move them around the obstacles. This activity gave the children an opportunity to practise giving precise instructions, which is the key skill for designing algorithms.

- We let the children randomly explore the *Hopscotch* app for about 15 minutes by just looking at the characters and sample games.

- We reminded the children that they would be creating a racing game using the *Hopscotch* app; therefore they needed to decide upon their characters and backgrounds. I asked them to draw their racing game design on paper, annotate it to show the actions required and then share it with others. Figure 8.1 is an example of a child's drawing with annotations. This was useful for those children who were having difficulties defining their ideas.

- In the second session we demonstrated how to write a script to make a background in *Hopscotch*. The children then practised creating their own background designs using *Hopscotch*.

**Figure 8.1** An example of a child's drawing with annotations

- We need to remember that children will have different cognitive abilities and be prepared to support those who would benefit from extra help or extra challenges. We provided a poster with instructions for creating a background, controlling the car using a button and programming the car on *Hopscotch* for those who needed extra support. Figure 8.2 is an example of an instruction guide for creating the Racing Cars game.

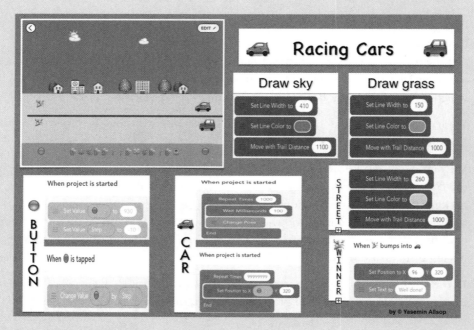

**Figure 8.2**  Instructions for Racing Cars project

- Once the children had written programs to create their backgrounds, we focused on how to write procedures for the buttons to control their characters that would be racing. This part of the lesson involved creating 'blue button', 'red button' and 'step' variables. An example of this procedure can be seen in Figure 8.3.

- Children tested what they had done so far and then debugged any problems that they detected in their programs.

- In the third session the children completed their programs and tested them to check that they worked. They exchanged games with a partner and made suggestions on how to make them better. We provided a challenge sheet for those who had finished and wanted to tinker with more complex ideas. Examples of these challenges can be seen in Table 8.1.

- In the fourth session, some children created a video presentation of their racing game combining narration and screenshots in *iMovie*. They shared their presentations with the whole class, which provided further discussion opportunities. We also looked at the vocabulary list on our working wall and talked about the new words that were added by the children during the sessions.

**Figure 8.3** An example procedure for 'red button' and 'red car'

## Assessment opportunities

Various methods were used for recording and assessing children's learning during this activity. Children were asked to take screenshots of their problems and annotate them to explain how they solved them using apps such as *Explain Everything* and *Keynote*. You can see an example of this in Figure 8.4. They were also asked to take screenshots of their games at different stages and create a video presentation at the end to share with the whole class. This helped them to regulate their own learning, as it enabled them to check on their progress throughout the activity. The game design activity also provided opportunities for group and whole class discussions, in which the children were able to reflect on their developing understanding of computer science concepts. Some of these discussions were recorded to evaluate their learning and identify the issues they faced. This evidence was then used to inform the planning of future sessions.

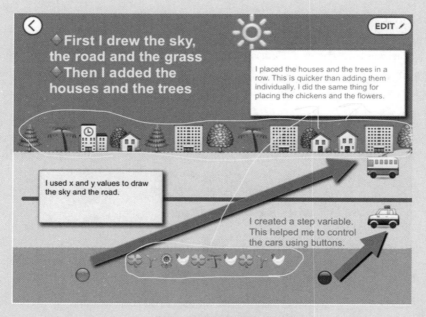

**Figure 8.4** An example of a child's annotations using the *Explain Everything* app

## Suggested activities using the Hopscotch app

Although our Racing Cars activity was aimed at Year 5 children, in coming years when children will have more experience of using different programming environments on tablets and computers, this activity might also be appropriate for lower Key Stage 2 classes. At our school we have begun to use *Hopscotch* in every age group from Year 3 upwards. Table 8.1 presents some activity ideas for teaching computer science concepts using *Hopscotch* across the year groups.

**Table 8.1** Activity ideas across age groups using the *Hopscotch* app

| Activity | Suitable for | Extension | Learning objective link to the National Curriculum |
|---|---|---|---|
| Change the appearance of characters on screen using blocks from the appearance palette. | YR 2, YR 3 | Write a script that moves a character. | Write a simple program to achieve specific goals. |
| Write a script that moves a character to the left and to the right by tilting the iPad. | YR 2, YR 3, YR 4 | Write a script that moves a character up and down by tilting the iPad. Move a character by changing x and y values. | Design and write a simple program to achieve specific goals. Use logical reasoning to predict the behaviour of simple programs. |
| Write a script that makes a character dance. Unplugged! Ask children to create a dance routine on paper and practise it with their friends first. | YR 3, YR 4 | Use more than one character to follow different dance routines using the 'repeat function'. | Write a simple program to achieve specific goals. Use repeat, sequence and selection in programs. |

| | | | |
|---|---|---|---|
| Create a script to tell a story. | YR 3, YR 4, YR 5 | Use more complex functions, e.g. rotating, changing x and y values, repeat, loop. Use more objects with different rules. | Use repeat, sequence and selection functions to write a simple program to achieve a specific goal. Understand what loops are and when and why they are used. |
| Write a script to program a character to draw shapes e.g. square, triangle. | YR 3, YR 4, YR 5, YR 6 | Provide children with codes for drawing shapes without repeat function. Ask them to simplify it using the repeat function. Ask children to write scripts for more complex shapes using 'rotate' command and 'repeat' function, e.g. hexagon. | Use logical reasoning to explain how some simple algorithms work. Write a simple program to achieve a specific goal. Design efficient procedures to simplify a program. Test programs and know when to debug. |
| Write a script to draw a simple maze background and design a solution to solve the maze. | YR 4, YR 5, YR 6 | Children create a script to write their name and code to utilise random colors and pen thickness. | Understand that computers can solve general problems and not just specific ones. Know how to use the 'random' block. Design, write and debug programs to achieve specific goals. |
| Use loops to draw a line drawing, e.g. a stick man or a star. | YR 4, YR 5, YR 6 | Learners take a screenshot of their drawing and exchange it with a partner. They invent an efficient solution to draw the shapes. | Understand loops and know when and why they are used. Use logical reasoning to explain how some simple algorithms work. |
| Write a script to design a game, e.g. Racing Cars. | YR 4, YR 5, YR 6 | Use a 'change value' block to make your character speed up as it moves. Make a timer for your game. Add a scoreboard to your game. | Design, write and debug programs to achieve specific goals. Use sequence, selection, and repetition in programs. Work with variables. |

Computer science has very strong links with mathematics and science, as well as design and technology, therefore it can be used to support children's learning in these disciplines. One example that we would like to mention here is the use of *LOGO* to teach children about directions, shapes and angels. *LOGO* is a programming language that was created in 1967 by Seymour Papert and Wally Feurzig for educational use. It was designed to enable young children to program the physical movement of a robot turtle and thereby teach programming concepts and thinking skills. In the *LOGO* environment children solve problems by programming the turtle to accomplish certain tasks and learning mainly takes place when children learn how to write instructions for the turtle to follow. Originally it was aimed to teach children both mathematical and programming concepts concurrently, however, it was quickly realised that *LOGO* could be used to teach skills in subject areas outside mathematics. There are many applications that continue to use the *LOGO* language. For example, *i-LOGO* is a mobile app on iPads which adopts a version of *LOGO*.

> **Activity**
>
> Look at the suggested activities in Table 8.2 and think about how you could use *i-LOGO* and apps that are listed in Table 8.3 to teach children computer science concepts linked to other curriculum areas.

**Table 8.2**   Suggested activities using *i-LOGO*

| Learning objectives: |
| --- |

- to use the properties of shapes to design algorithms for drawing regular polygons;
- to use logical reasoning to explain how some simple algorithms work;
- to use sequence, selection and repetition in programs.

| Task 1: Discuss procedures for using *LOGO* to draw circles, triangles and squares. Talk about how knowing about the properties of shapes such as angles, corners and sides helps us with writing programs. | |
| --- | --- |
| Draw a triangle | Repeat 3 [forward 100 turn right 120] |
| Draw a square | Repeat 4 [forward 100 turn right 90] |
| Draw a circle | Repeat 360 [forward 1 turn right 1] |
| Draw a right-angled triangle | Forward 60 right 150 forward 69 right 120 |
| | Forward 34 right 90 |
| Draw a semi-circle | Repeat 45 [forward 1 right 4] |

| Task 2: Show learners pictures of shapes drawn using *i-LOGO*. Ask them to come up with scripts to create these shapes. Remind them to use properties of the shapes to help them, e.g. angles, corners and number of sides. | |
| --- | --- |
| | How do you create this shape? |
| Write a procedure that writes the word 'Logo'. | How do you create this shape? |

| Task 3: Provide learners with instructions. Can you predict which shape it will produce? | |
| --- | --- |
| What will happen if you try:<br><br>Repeat 4 [forward 100 right 90]<br><br>Repeat 3 [forward 100 right 120]<br><br>Repeat 8 [forward 40 right 45] | |

# Discussion

## Key terms

You will find it useful to familiarise yourself with these key computing terms so that you can make them part of your classroom vocabulary, enabling children to discuss their learning.

- *Algorithm*: an algorithm is a set of precise instructions to solve a problem or achieve a goal.
- *Debugging*: identifying and removing errors from scripts and programs.
- *Decomposition*: tackling larger problems by breaking them into smaller parts so that we can explain the process either to someone or to a computer.

- *Abstraction*: the process of removing or reducing details from a complex object to facilitate focus on relevant concepts.

- *Iteration*: computers repeat similar tasks without making any errors. Repeated execution of a sequence of statements is called iteration, e.g. loops.

- *Generalisation*: transferring a problem-solving process to a wide range of problems.

- *Procedures*: block of code that performs a specific task.

- *Variable*: a value, which can change depending on conditions. Variables used for holding on to a value to use it later.

- *Loops*: a sequence of instructions that repeats until a specific task is achieved.

- i: an instruction in a program that is only executed when a specific condition is met.

## A constructionist approach

The adoption of tablet technology in schools in the UK is still in its infancy and the use of tablets for teaching computer science is a relatively new concept. Rather than focusing purely on mobile learning, we will explore the potential of tablets for teaching computing concepts in relation to the constructionist teaching approach. For this we first need to define computer science and computational thinking.

Computer science (CS) is the study of how computers and computational processes work and how they are designed. Computer scientists create algorithms to transform information and abstractions into model complex systems. The most important skill for a computer scientist is problem solving. Problem solving involves formulating problems, thinking creatively about solutions, and designing a clear solution. Teaching children to think like a computer scientist helps them to understand how computers think when solving problems, which in turn promotes computational thinking. According to Wing, computational thinking is a:

> *thought process involved in formulating problems and their solutions so that the solutions are represented in a form that can be effectively carried out by an information-processing agent.*

(Wing, 2010)

Based on the ability to think logically, algorithmically and recursively, computational thinking involves knowledge of the fundamentals of computing such as algorithm, abstraction, iteration and generalisation. It also includes logical reasoning, problem decomposition, testing, debugging and visualisation skills. Developing these skills enables students to represent and solve problems computationally in any discipline and in daily life. When supported with a constructionist teaching approach, as we outline below, children's interaction with digital tools, such as tablets, provides a context for children to develop computational thinking, as it offers a space to practise and develop metacognitive problem-solving and reasoning skills (Clements and Meredith, 1992).

Before exploring constructionism, it is appropriate to discuss constructivism, as the two approaches are very much interrelated. Championed by John Dewey (1938) and developed by Jean Piaget (1970), constructivism is a learning theory that focuses on knowledge and explores how people learn. It suggests that people construct meaning through their interactions and experiences in social environments. It also stresses the importance of prior knowledge in learning and how previous experiences shape subsequent actions. Learning therefore is all about learners adjusting their mental model to accommodate new experiences.

One of the key elements of the constructivist theory of learning suggests that children learn by doing. Children construct new knowledge about the physical and social worlds in which they live, through playful interaction with objects and people. Children do not need to be forced to learn; they are motivated by their own desire to make sense of their world (Piaget, 1970; Piaget and Inhelder, 1969). According to Piaget, children learn when they are actively involved in the process (Slavin, 1994). The teacher's role in traditional classrooms is seen as the sole giver of knowledge and the student's role is that of a passive receiver. The constructivist approach encourages children to take an active part in learning by using their ideas and interests to drive the learning process. The role of the teacher in this model is to support children when they need it and guide them to take control of their self-directed learning experiences (Ringstaff *et al.*, 1991).

Vygosky's constructivism (1978) is known as social constructivism because he stressed the importance of the social context and culture within the learning process. He described learning as a collaborative activity and explained the significance the role of history and the social environment bear in acquiring new knowledge. Learning takes place when children interact with the social environment and internalise their experience. Vygotsky (1978) suggests that cognitive development is limited to a certain range at a particular age. However, with the help of social interaction, such as assistance from a teacher, students can understand concepts that they cannot know on their own.

Influenced by Piaget's (1954) constructivism, Papert's (1991) work with children and digital tools led him to develop his pedagogical theory of 'constructionism', which states that children actively construct knowledge through experience, described as 'learning-by-doing'. As mentioned before, Papert and Feurzeig (1967) created the *LOGO* programming language that could be used by young children to move and rotate a floor turtle. Papert (1985) suggested that the turtle is 'good to think with' and helps children to develop their problem-solving skills through designing solutions, which could also enhance their cognitive development. Kafai (1995) observed children using *LOGO* and suggested that when children make their own computational artefacts, they can take control of their own learning and develop their own ideas.

From a constructionist perspective then, learning happens when learners actually engage in the act of producing something. Using apps on tablets for learning to program or making games provides an important opportunity for children to practise problem-solving skills as students actively construct their own computational artefacts. Looking at our case study, where children created their own racing game using the *Hopscotch* app, it is clear that this task required the children to design, visualise and investigate solutions, which led them to develop computational thinking. In this scenario, the role of the teacher is to empower and support learners to take control of their learning by defining and developing ownership of a problem to investigate, so that they design their own projects and collaboratively build their knowledge.

Papert (1987) suggests that this process is not as simple as learners just taking an active role; rather, educators need to design learning environments and make tools available to the learners to accommodate their active participation in their learning. He refers to computers as powerful tools that provide a context and opportunities for children to understand abstract concepts from an early age. He presents a new kind of learning environment, where the focus is on the process of inventing 'objects-to-think-with' that underline the interaction between children and computers (Papert, 1987). Whilst designing their racing game using *Hopscotch*, our children were active participants, building knowledge through writing, testing and debugging their scripts. In this learning scenario, the tablets became 'powerful tools' and the apps provided a space for children to interact with abstract concepts and take control of their own learning. Through game design activities using tablets, the children created their own knowledge of the world by creating objects; in our case they were making games, experimenting with ideas, modifying them and studying how they operated.

## Developing metacognitive awareness through computer game design

Computer game design as a computational activity provides a context for students to invent, develop and use metacognitive strategies. Cross and Paris (1988) defined metacognition as the knowledge and control children have over their own thinking and learning activities. In our experience, students can improve their learning by being aware of their own thinking and regulating their learning activities accordingly. Claxton (1999) explains metacognition as a way of supporting people to manage their minds more productively, which then enables them to use their resources more effectively.

Sternberg (1998, p17) expands on this by suggesting that metacognitive abilities are driven by motivation, which activates learning and thinking skills, and then feeds back into the metacognitive skills, enabling a learner's level of expertise to increase. According to Sternberg (1998) these processes include planning, evaluating and monitoring problem-solving activities and allocating cognitive resources appropriately. Sternberg's analysis of metacognitive behaviours in problem-solving activities has seven stages: problem recognition, problem definition, problem representation, formulation of solution strategy, allocation of resources, monitoring and evaluation. A number of studies similarly describe planning, monitoring and evaluation as the main metacognitive skills (Fisher, 2005; Schraw *et al.*, 2006; Whitebread *et al.*, 2009).

Flavell (1979) listed exploring, setting goals, organising, planning, self-questioning, choosing and applying, monitoring and managing thinking as metacognitive skills.

We will consider 'planning', 'evaluating' and 'monitoring' as the main metacognitive strategies relevant to our unit of work. We will also include 'processing' as a metacognitive regulating-application skill representing the strategy of monitoring problem-solving activities and the deployment of cognitive resources.

### Metacognitive planning

Planning skills help children to formulate their actions in order to reach their goals. They provide learners with a base for analysing their approaches to a task before they actually start working on it. Planning involves exploring, analysing, designing, engineering, visualising and experimenting. In our programming and computer game design context, students had to think about the title of their game, their narration, characters, backgrounds and so forth. They asked questions such as: What is my task/my goal? What do I need to know and what strategies do I need to use? What are the steps for making my computer game?

### Metacognitive processing

Processing can be a cognitive or a metacognitive strategy depending on the purpose of its use and also whether the activity is directed at the 'self'. It involves behaviours such as conversational thinking, connecting, monitoring problem solving, selecting strategies, and making decisions. According to Vygotsky (1986), language and thought dwell together. He believed that in order to raise awareness of mental activities, a learner needs to know how to articulate their thoughts. He saw dialogic exchange as an essential skill, which can transform the way in which children think and learn. We can trace the origins of the use of dialogue for learning to Socratic learning. In a Socratic learning context, language was seen as a social inquiry tool (Nelson, 1949). Bruner (1986) describes language as 'a way of sorting one's thoughts about things.' Asking questions of the 'self' or 'others' does not aim to evaluate what a child already knows; rather it enables them to analyse, reflect, share and extend their understanding and thinking. Articulating their thoughts through language in this way, learners' begin to regulate their mental activities when designing solutions; they make decisions and classify or select appropriate strategies to accomplish a task. This conversation element makes 'thought' more visible and manageable. In this domain, conversation becomes a strategy to negotiate meaning rather than a tool to communicate. Whilst making computer games, learners posed questions, which helped them to define the best strategies to solve a problem. For example during our game design activities, the children asked questions such as, 'Which strategy shall I use?', 'What is the problem here?', 'How can I solve this problem?', 'What does my partner think?' and 'What do you think about my solution?'

### Metacognitive monitoring

Monitoring refers to a learners' ability to manage their own cognitive skills while working on a task to identify the problems and modify their planning as needed. It is a difficult strategy to develop and use, even by adults, as it requires an awareness of one's own progress. Testing a sequence of codes to check if a game works is an example. The questions learners asked were: 'Am I on the right track?', 'Do I understand the task?', 'Am I working towards my goals?', 'Is my plan working?', and 'Do I need to make any changes to my planning?'

### Metacognitive evaluating

The evaluation skill is all about learners reflecting on their own progress by checking the final outcome against their objective. It involves auditing the solutions they have designed and the strategies they used to execute their planning for a specific goal. The questions that were asked by the learners were: 'Have I reached my target?', 'Which strategies worked?', 'Which methods didn't work?' and 'What could I do to make it better?'

## Activity

### Choosing and evaluating apps for teaching computer science

Most of the apps for teaching computer science are available on iPads and only a few are available on the Android platform. It is important for teachers to evaluate the apps in terms of age suitability, accessibility and their relevance to the teaching context. Involving children in the app evaluation process can also be useful, as it helps them to reflect on their own views and understanding. Table 8.3 presents a suggested list of apps for teaching computer science available on iPads and Android tablets.

**Table 8.3** A list of apps for teaching computer science

| App | Platform | What it does | Suitable for |
|---|---|---|---|
| ALEX | iPad | A puzzle game in which you program ALEX the robot to complete tasks using sequences of commands. | KS 1, KS 2 |
| Bee-Bot | iPad/iPhone/iPod Touch | The Bee-Bot app teaches children directional language and programming through sequences of forwards, backwards, left and right 90-degree turns. | KS 1 |
| Cargo-bot | iPad | A puzzle game where you teach a robot how to move crates. | KS 1, KS 2 |
| Cato's Hike | iPad | A puzzle game which introduces programming using loops, branches, 'if/else' and 'go to' labels. | KS 1, KS 2 |
| Daisy the Dinosaur | iPad | An easy to use drag-and-drop programming app that teaches children basic sequencing, loops and events through built-in challenges. | KS 1 |
| Lego Fixthefactory | iPad/Android | A puzzle game for teaching programming. | KS 1, KS 2 |
| Hakitzu Elite | iPad and Android | This app teaches the basics of JavaScript by programming robots to fight their opponent. | KS 2 |
| Hopscotch | iPad | A drag-and-drop interactive programming environment for creating animations, stories and games. | KS 1, KS 2 |

| i-LOGO | iPad | A version of *LOGO* that was created in 1967. It has a functional programming capability with global and local variables. | KS 2 |
|---|---|---|---|
| Kinescript | iPad | A visual drag-and-drop programming app with built-in characters, background and a sound library. | KS 2 |
| Kodable | iPad | A game for introducing programming concepts and problem solving. | KS 1 |
| Lightbot | iPad/iPhone/iPod Touch/Android | Teaches programming concepts through puzzle games. | KS 2 |
| Move the turtle | iPhone/iPad | Similar to *LOGO*, a turtle for introducing basic programming concepts. | KS 2 |
| RoboLogic 2 HD | iPad | Program a robot's movements by dragging commands to the memory of the bot. Create and call re-usable functions to achieve the goal. | KS 2 |
| Scratch Junior | iPad | Children program characters to move, dance and sing by snapping programming blocks. | KS 1 |

## Activity

Using the table above, identify one app for Key Stage 1 and one for Key Stage 2 that you would like to explore with children. Test them out and make a note of how you could incorporate them into a set of lessons, how you could differentiate for abilities and which computational thinking skills you might reinforce.

## Summary and Key Points

Apps on tablets can provide some excellent opportunities for teaching elements of computer science when they are combined with well-designed activities. It is important for teachers to evaluate the apps carefully in relation to learning objectives and define which apps can be used for developing specific computational thinking concepts. One way of doing this is by creating a scheme of work to show progression across the age groups and conceptual development in learning. We also need to be aware that just giving children tablets and allowing them to use apps for game design, problem solving and programming activities does not guarantee that they will make progress. The learning environment needs to be designed efficiently for students to actively manage their own learning and provide opportunities for talk and collaborative activities.

Teaching computational thinking, which is based on designing solutions for problems, is more than just transmitting the knowledge of coding. Teachers should allow learners to experiment with ideas and use purposeful questioning and specific tasks to guide learners in constructing their own knowledge. For this, it is important for teachers to have the required subject knowledge and understanding of pedagogical approaches that work well. Furthermore, using different assessment strategies, not just at the end of the activity, but throughout the sessions, will help learners to ensure that they are on the right track. This will also enable teachers to keep a record of children's learning, which is very valuable for informing the planning of the future sessions.

## Reflective Questions

Our game design activity provided opportunities for reflective group and whole class discussions. How could you extend this to other computing lessons?

We have focused on games design in this chapter. How might you apply some of these skills to design learning games across other areas of the curriculum?

How might you present the positive learning outcomes of your computing lessons to parents and governors?

## Useful Links

**http://code-it.co.uk** (accessed 20 December 2014).

This site provides activity ideas on programming with *Logo, Scratch* and *Python* for Key Stage 2, as well as plans for other aspects of ICT.

**http://csunplugged.org** (accessed 20 December 2014).

A collection of free learning activities that teach computer science through engaging games and puzzles.

**www.softronix.com/logo.html** (accessed 20 December 2014).

A free and well-supported version of *LOGO* with a Windows interface.

**https://slp.somerset.gov.uk/cypd/elim/somersetict/Site%20Pages/Computing%20Curriculum%20 Primary/Primary_Computing_home.aspx?PageView=Shared** (accessed 20 December 2014).

A computing curriculum for primary learners. This website has many useful resources and planning guides for teaching the computing curriculum.

## App List for the Chapter

*ALEX, Bee-Bot, Cargo-bot, Cato's Hike, Daisy the Dinosaur, Lego Fixthefactory, Hakitzu Elite, Hopscotch, i-LOGO, Kinescript, Kodable, Lightbot, Move the turtle, RoboLogic 2 HD, Scratch jr.*

## Further Reading

Resnick, M and Rosenbaum, E (2013) Designing for tinkerability, in Honey, M and Kanter, D (eds) *Design, Make, Play: Growing the Next Generation of STEM Innovators*, pp. 163–81. London: Routledge.

In this chapter Mitchel Resnick and Eric Rosenbaum discuss the relation between tinkerability and computation. They suggest that computational construction kits and activities encourage designing and tinkering with computation in which children not only develop mathematical, engineering and computational ideas, but also learn to think creatively and work collaboratively. This chapter is a must for understanding how children develop computational thinking through design and tinkering with ideas.

Harel, I and Papert, S (1991) *CONSTRUCTIONISM*, Ablex Publishing Corporation.

New technologies continue to enter into our classrooms. As educators, knowing strategies that will work well when implementing the use of these emerging tools is very important. Constructionism, which focuses on 'learning-by-making', where learners actively construct knowledge, is one of the main theories that support the effective use of technology in teaching and learning. This book provides the theoretical knowledge that is required for understanding how children learn and make sense of the world around them when learning with technology.

Berry, M (2014) There is more to the new computing curriculum than just coding. Available from: **http://milesberry.net/2014/05/there-is-more-to-the-new-computing-curriculum-than-just-coding** (accessed 20 December 2014).

Since the announcement of the new computing curriculum, the majority of the headlines have been about teaching children how to code. This can be misleading, as computer science is not just about coding. In this article Miles Berry explains computer science and how it relates to programming and coding in a very flowing and clear way. This article is very useful for understanding the context of computer science in the new computer curriculum.

# References

Bruner, J (1986) *Actual Minds, Possible Worlds*. Cambridge, MA: Harvard University Press.

Claxton, G (1999) *Wise Up: The Challenge of Lifelong Learning*. London: Bloomsbury.

Clements, DH and Meredith, JS (1992) *Research on Logo: Effects and efficacy*. Available from: **http://el.media.mit.edu/logo-foundation/pubs/papers/research_logo.html** (accessed 16 August 2014).

Cross, DR and Paris, SG (1988) Developmental and instructional analyses of children's metacognition and reading comprehension, *Journal of Educational Psychology*, 80(2), 131–42.

Dewey, J (1938) *Experience and Education*. New York: Simon & Schuster.

Dwyer, D, Ringstaff, C and Sandholtz, J (1991) Changes in teachers' beliefs and practices in technology-rich classrooms, *Educational Leadership*, 48( 8).

Feurzeig, W and Papert, S (1967) The Logo Programming Language. Available from: **http://el.media.mit.edu/logo-foundation/logo/programming.html** (accessed 17 August 2014).

Fisher, R (2005) (2nd ed) *Teaching Children to Think*. Cheltenham: Nelson Thornes.

Flavell, JH (1979) Metacognition and cognitive monitoring: A new area of cognitive-developmental inquiry. *American Psychologist*, 34, 906–11.

Kafai, YB (1995) *Minds in Play: Computer game design as a context for children's learning*. Mahwah, NJ: Lawrence Erlbaum.

Nelson, L (1949) *Socratic Method and Critical Philosophy*. New Haven, CT: Yale University

Papert, S (1985) Different visions of Logo. *Computers in the Schools*, 2(2–3): 3–8. Available from: **http://dx.doi.org/10.1300/J025v02n02_02** (accessed 16 August 2014).

Papert, S (1987) *A Critique of Technocentrism in Thinking about the School of the Future*. Available from: **www.papert.org/articles/ACritiqueofTechnocentrism.html** (accessed 15 August 2014).

Papert, S (1991) Situating constructionism, in Harel, I and Papert, S (eds) *Constructionism*. Norwood, NJ: Ablex Publishing Corporation.

Piaget, J (1954) *The Construction of Reality in the Child*. New York: Ballantine.

Piaget, J (1970) *Logic and Psychology*. New York: Basic Books.

Piaget, J and Inhelder, B (1969) *The Psychology of the Child*. New York: Basic Books.

Schraw, G, Crippen, KJ and Hartley, K (2006) Promoting self-regulation in science education: Metacognition as part of a broader perspective on learning. *Research in Science Education*, 36, 111–39.

Sternberg, RJ (1998) Abilities are forms of developing expertise. *Educational Researcher*, 27(3), 11–20.

Vygotsky, S (1978) Interaction between learning and development. *Mind in Society*, pp79–91 [online]. Available from: **www.psy.cmu.edu/~siegler/vygotsky78.pdf** (accessed 16 August 2014).

Whitebread, D, Coltman, P, Pino Pasternak, D, Sangster, C, Grau, V, Bingham, S, Almeqdad, Q and Demetriou, D (2009) The development of two observational tools for assessing metacognition and self-regulated learning in young children. *Metacognition and Learning*, 4(1), 63–85.

Wing, J (2006) Computational thinking. *Communications of the ACM*, 49(3), 33–5.

Wing, JM (2010) Computational thinking: What and why? *Link Magazine*. Available from: **www.cs.cmu.edu/%7ECompThink/papers/TheLinkWing.pdf** (accessed 18 August 2014).

# Chapter 9

# Creating your own apps

## Introduction

In this chapter we will go beyond using apps to develop coding skills by building your own apps that you can share and use on your mobile devices. There are a number of easy to use programs that allow you to build apps using simple visual programming languages. Two of the leaders in the field of app building for education are Microsoft Research's *TouchDevelop* (**www.touchdevelop.com**) and MIT's (Massachusetts Institute of Technology) *App Inventor2* (**http://ai2.appinventor.mit.edu**). These are both free to use. You can use these to create apps using a PC or Apple, Microsoft and Android platforms and, as both systems are cloud based, you can create and use your apps across devices. For example, you could create an app on one device and then continue developing on another, opening up the possibility for children to continue with their projects outside the classroom. Although the *TouchDevelop* and *App Innovator* apps are only available for Android mobile devices, you can use the browser on a PC, Mac, iPad or iPhone to both build and play the apps and share with the online community.

*App Inventor* was originally developed by Google who then sold it to MIT's Centre for Mobile Learning for further development. Their version, the *App Inventor2*, was released in 2012. Mitch Resnick is part of this team; he also helped to develop the popular coding program *Scratch* (**http://scratch.mit.edu**) and when you start using *App Inventor2* you will see very similar blocks of visual codes that can be dragged and clicked into place.

In this chapter we will focus on the *TouchDevelop* app creator, which can also be used via the browser on your PC or tablet. This free to use visual programming environment is developed by Microsoft Research. It can provide a transition from visual programming in *Scratch* to text-based programming between Key Stages 2 and 3. The environment allows you to pick suggested commands and search for commands; it also provides hints for next steps and to help you identify bugs.

If you have not used either of these systems and would like to learn, both *TouchDevelop* and *App Inventor2* have easy to follow online tutorials created by the developers. You can find some links at the end of the chapter.

## Learning Objectives

At the end of this chapter you should be able to:

- have an understanding of how to use *TouchDevelop* to teach the primary computing national curriculum;
- transfer your skills developed in other visual programs to write a simple app;
- support children to develop a simple app.

## Links to Teachers' Standards

The following Teachers' Standards are particularly relevant to this chapter:

TS1 Establish a safe and stimulating environment for pupils.
Set goals that stretch and challenge pupils of all backgrounds, abilities and dispositions.
TS2 Demonstrate knowledge and understanding of how pupils learn and how this impacts on teaching.
Encourage pupils to take a responsible and conscientious attitude to their own work and study.
TS3 Promote a love of learning and children's intellectual curiosity.
Set homework and plan other out-of-class activities to consolidate and extend the knowledge and understanding pupils have acquired.
Contribute to the design and provision of an engaging curriculum within the relevant subject area(s).

The following criteria from Computing at Schools Computing Progression Pathways are particularly relevant to this chapter:

### Yellow (Key Stage 2)

- designs simple algorithms using loops, and selection, i.e. 'if' statements; Algorithmic Thinking (**AL**);
- uses logical reasoning to predict outcomes (**AL**);
- detects and corrects errors, i.e. debugging, in algorithms (**AL**);
- uses arithmetic operators, if statements, and loops, within programs (**AL**);
- uses logical reasoning to predict the behaviour of programs (**AL**);
- detects and corrects simple semantic errors, i.e. debugging, in programs (**AL**).

### Orange (Key Stage 3)

- designs solutions (algorithms) that use repetition and two-way selection, i.e. 'if', 'then' and 'else' (**AL**);
- uses logical reasoning to predict outputs, showing an awareness of inputs (**AL**);
- creates programs that implement algorithms to achieve given goals (**AL**);
- declares and assigns variables; Abstraction (**AB**);
- uses post-tested loop, e.g. 'until', and a sequence of selection statements in programs, including an 'if', 'then' and 'else' statement (**AL**).

Before you can start these activities, you will need to set up a *TouchDevelop* account. This is simple. Go to the *TouchDevelop* homepage at **www.touchdevelop.com**, where you can choose a number of ways to sign in: Microsoft account, Facebook, Google and Yahoo. You may need to refer to your school's e-safety policy if the pupils are to have their own accounts. Your username may be auto generated, but you can change this using Account Settings.

The key areas that we will be using are in the home screen or Hub, and are the My Scripts and the Learn areas. The environment looks very similar to the Windows 8 interface. All of the scripts or programs that you write will be saved in My Scripts and, so long as you sign into *TouchDevelop*, you can access all your scripts no matter which device you use. The Learn area is where you can access tutorials.

# Example from practice

*Turtle challenge: drawing shapes*

In the
classroom

## Context

If you have used *Textease Turtle*, *Scratch* or something similar, you will probably recognise this activity. You can also find a tutorial in the *TouchDevelop* online course that covers elements of this activity. I find that using a familiar activity like the Turtle is a good way to help pupils to find their way around new environments. If children are familiar with the concepts of programming the Turtle to draw a shape they can focus on how the *TouchDevelop* environment works.

This activity can be delivered in a number of ways. For Key Stage 1, I would use the interactive whiteboard (IWB) and demonstrate this as a different programming language, with the children discussing the process and making predictions. As the children move into Key Stage 2, I would use the Turtle Challenge so that children work more independently, probably in a group, to program their own app that they can share online. This activity can be further differentiated by asking more able children to program their Turtle to draw more complex shapes. As *TouchDevelop* is web based, children can log into their *TouchDevelop* account and continue working on their apps at home.

---

### Learning Outcomes

The pupil will be able to:

- predict the outcome of running of the script (KS1);
- programme a Turtle in *TouchDevelop* to draw a square (KS2);
- recognise key programming features in TouchDevelop (KS2);
- use simple loops in programming (KS2);
- modify variables in a simple programme (KS2);
- publish their app (KS2).

---

## Outline

In the My Scripts area you will see an option to Create Script; when you click on it you are asked if you would like to select a template; if you choose a blank script it will take you to a script editing page.

The panel on the left provides some key functions: a back button to return to the Hub, a run button to run your programs and, most important, an undo button in case you make a mistake.

The central panel is the Script Explorer, where you can search for actions. And the panel on the right is the code window, where you write your code or script. As you start writing your script, some action buttons appear at the bottom as illustrated in the earlier image. If you are working on a mobile device the screen may look different as the Edit Window takes up most of the screen when Script Explorer is collapsed.

---

## Activity

### Turtle challenge

- From the My Scripts area select Create a Script.
- From the scripts template select Blank Turtle.
- Click into the coding window below 'action main' into 'do nothing'. You will notice that the line on the left of the script turns red. This indicates that there is an error or something that needs to be done. When you click in the coding window the Action Options buttons appear at the bottom of the screen. Select Turtle.
- Just like other coding packages like *Textease Turtle* you need to tell the Turtle what to do; select the action → forward (0); you can select this either from the action buttons at the bottom of the screen or use the search function in the Script Explorer area. As you select this, you will notice that hints on how to handle this action will appear just above the action buttons. *TouchDevelop* constantly gives you hints as you move through the process.
- You need to enter how many steps you want the Turtle to take. When I demonstrate this activity, this is where I take the opportunity to have conversations with the children about how far this will make the Turtle move, which gives you a chance to compare the Turtle's actions to units of measure and make predictions about how far it will move.
- Click into the plus sign below the 'Turtle → forward (50)', which will give you the next line so that you can enter the next instruction, which is 'insert →turn left (0)'; as we are drawing a square, we will need to either enter 90 or we can express it as 360/4. Again, here, I use this as an opportunity to have conversations about the size of the angle for various shapes and the relationship between the number of sides and the dominator used for 360, and why we are using 360.

---

I carry on discussing what we need to tell the Turtle to do so that it can draw a square, often getting children to walk through the instructions to test them out. I then either enter their instructions or allow them to do it for themselves. You do not need to worry about them getting it right the first time. If the Turtle does not do what they expect, it is really important to get them to debug their algorithm.

To make a square you will need to instruct the Turtle to move forward, for example:

Forward 200 steps and Turn Left $90^0$ four times.

Enter these instructions into the code window. Ask your pupils to suggest ways to simplify the code. This is an opportunity to introduce the concept of abstraction.

You can do this by inserting a 'for' loop around one set of → forward (0) →turn left (0), indicating that you want the Turtle to repeat the action four times.

I use this Turtle activity as a foundation for exploring other shapes such as creating a square spiral or a square 'S' shape.

*Creating a simple game*

# Context

By the time that most pupils reach upper Key Stage 2, with some experience in coding, they are ready to create simple games. *TouchDevelop* can help to make the links between visual and text-based coding languages, providing the transition into Key Stage 3. There are a number of online tutorials developed by *TouchDevelop* and on *YouTube* that provide clear instructions on how to create simple games (**www.touchdevelop.com/docs/tutorials**).

The task of creating a game can be handled in a number of ways. You could demonstrate the whole process as a directed task where you clearly outline the steps to your pupils, perhaps providing them with a worksheet to work through. The *TouchDevelop* website has some examples available to support this. You could also set it as a more independent task, where the pupils work using their own knowledge of coding or using the online tutorials on their own to create the app. This independent approach would particularly suit situations where you want to add stretch and challenge to those already comfortable with coding in *TouchDevelop* or as an activity in a coding club. I tend to make my decision on how I am going to approach this activity based on the individuals in the group and will often alter it depending on how pupils respond. I find it useful to remember that just because I may be intimidated by something like coding does not necessarily mean that my pupils will be; it is after all part of their everyday life.

Before you get started it is useful to consider the basic requirements for a game. You need to start with an idea or 'story board' for the game. This will inform the basic elements that you need to create:

* background;

* Sprite;

* actions for the Sprite;

* conditions within the game (such as timing, scoring, gravity and lives).

I like to get pupils to think about the computer games that they play and make a list of the features of a 'good' game, so that they can use that to plan their own game. You will need to manage their expectations, as they will be building a simple game. I get them to look at some of the featured apps in the Showcase in the *TouchDevelop* Hub as examples. When you select an app in the Hub, this will give you a screen where you can Run the script, and, by selecting Edit, you can examine the script. This gives you the chance to get children to predict from the script how the game will play, as well as getting them to evaluate the games against their list of 'good features'. I will often ask the class to pick the top three games, so that we can look more closely at the script for them to predict which lines of script relate to which activity and encourage them to change features such as the variables so that they can see the impact on the game.

As part of this planning process I also get pupils to write a plan for their game with all the elements that they would like to include, and then get them to think about how they will code each of these. It is good practice to use tracking sheets similar to the one illustrated so that they can use the first three columns as they plan and the last two columns to record their activity. This helps to make the debugging process more visible.

**Table 9.1**   Planning to program a game

| Object | What I want the object to do? | The script to do this | What happened when I tried this? | What changes do I need to make? |
|--------|-------------------------------|-----------------------|----------------------------------|----------------------------------|
| Turtle | Move Forward | ♻ turtle → forward (0) | It didn't move | Add how far I want it to move |

I find that pupils learn more if they work out the solution or debug the code themselves. If they struggle, I encourage them to ask others in the class using an 'Ask three then me' approach. I then open the question up to the whole class to discuss possible strategies rather than giving them the answer straight away. This way, they can see themselves and their peers as having the ability to work out the solutions for themselves. They are then able to experience that greater feeling of reward when they have worked hard for the solution. The success of this approach is, of course, dependent on having created an atmosphere where it is acceptable to take risks and sometimes to make mistakes in the process of achieving the goal.

---

**Learning Objectives**

Our intended learning objectives are for the pupil to be able:

- to write the script for a background to a simple game;
- to write the script for an animated sprite for a simple game;
- to debug a script for a simple game;
- to publish their simple game app.

---

# Outline

Here is a breakdown of creating a simple game where you have a sprite that moves with gravity to the bottom of the screen and, when you tap the sprite, it makes a noise and bounces up. If the sprite hits the bottom of the screen, you lose a life and when the sprite hits the side it bounces back.

This activity is based on one of the Tutorials in the Learn area of the Hub, so you can easily use that to help you as you plan your own sessions.

The images that you use in the app can be selected from the Script Explorer by selecting 'Add new action or event'. This gives you an option to select images already saved within *TouchDevelop*, images from the web or upload your own images. When you choose images from the web you will need to ensure that you use copyright free images. You can save online images that have a Creative Commons licence by using the Google Advanced search settings. Alternatively, you can take your own photographs or create your own images and upload those. As you save your image into *TouchDevelop*, you are given the option to remove the white background, which they advise for sprites. You are reminded that 'Everyone will be able to see your picture on the internet forever', which offers a great opportunity to reinforce the concept of e-safety.

When we are developing games, I get my pupils to create their own sprite using *PowerPoint*, as I find this a good environment to manipulate shapes to create creatures. The activity also addresses the statements in the National Curriculum related to using technology to create and manipulate content. Children can then use the Save As function in *PowerPoint* to save the current slide as a .png file and then upload it into *TouchDevelop*. Creating their own sprite has the advantage of contextualising the game. You could also download sound files for the game in the same way. I find that it is easier to create and save these elements as usable assets before starting to write the scripts in *TouchDevelop*.

Once you have your images sorted, from the My Scripts area select Create a script. Then select a Games Template. Upload your saved images by clicking on the 'Add new action, event … ' in the Script Explorer area.

You are now ready to write the script. Here is an outline that describes the actions that you need to take, alongside what the script should look like in the Edit Window.

**Table 9.2** Scripting a game

| Description of actions | Script in the Code Window |
|---|---|
| Background: select 'Wall' then → set background picture, art select an image (underwater or space). You can use: | **action** main () <br> **var** board := ♻game→ start <br> wall→ set background picture(✿ Space Background 5) |
| Sprite: select board → create picture, art select image (fish or alien) | **var** sprite := board→ create picture(✿ monster_1) |
| Set the size of sprite. | sprite→ set width(100) |
| Action for the Sprite: <br> when sprite is tapped, it <br> moves upwards (y axis is positive moving down) <br> Make a sound: <br> every time it's touched you score 100 points. | sprite→ on tap(tapped) <br> **where** tapped(x : Number , y : Number) **is** <br> sprite→ set speed y( - 200) <br> ✿ Pikachu sound→ play <br> ♻game→ add score(100) <br> **end** |
| Set the gravity: <br> get the sprite to bounce when it goes below the board. | board→ set gravity(0, 400) <br> board→ add on every frame(perform) <br> **where** perform() **is** |

*(Continued)*

**Table 9.2** (Continued)

| Description of actions | Script in the Code Window |
|---|---|
| Making a squashing sound. Bounce up in a random fashion. Lose a life if sprite drops below screen. If the sprite hits the side then it bounces back making a sound. | **if** sprite→ y › board→ height **then**<br>sprite→ set speed y( - 500)<br>✿ squash→ play<br>**var** x2 := math→ random range( - 100, 100) * 3<br>sprite→ set speed x(x2)<br>game→ remove life(1)<br>**else** do nothing **end** if<br>**if** sprite→ x ‹ 0 **or** sprite→ x › board→ width **then**<br>sprite→ set speed x( - sprite→ speed x)<br>**var** snd := ✿ squash<br>**else** do nothing **end** if<br>**end**<br>**end** action |

Once the apps have been completed, when you select the script from your Hub you will be taken to a page that offers a number of useful options.

When you choose to Publish, you are reminded about storing passwords and confidential information within the script as the app will be on the internet forever, which offers another opportunity to reinforce e-safety and responsible use of the internet. Publish generates a link that you can either cut and paste or use the buttons to share through e-mail or social media.

Selecting Code will display the code, and if you scroll to the bottom you are given an option to Print/e-mail allowing you to save the script and you can include that in a record of progress.

As you start working with *TouchDevelop* you will see that there is much potential to use this coding environment to extend pupils' learning. In our example we used a script to recreate gravity. There are a number of other physics-based actions, such as velocity, and one of the templates on offer is Physics Game Starter, which provides the environment which will set gravity as a default option.

# Discussion

## The computing curriculum

The introduction of the 2014 computing curriculum has led to a great deal of debate in the educational and wider communities. Concerns have been raised, for example, about the appropriateness of teaching 'programming' or 'coding' to young children. I suspect that some of these disagreements may be linked to the interpretation of the terms used rather than the intent of the programme of study. An interpretation suggested by Resnick (2013), which I find useful, is to think about computing in the same way that we consider literacy and numeracy for children. We would not expect a child in Key Stage 1 to be able to write a screenplay; however, we do understand that in order to be able to write or understand the concept of a screenplay, at some time you need to develop fundamental literacy skills. And we agree that these literacy skills give you the potential to produce and engage with a range of texts throughout your life. We would not dream of suggesting that children should not have opportunities to develop literacy skills from birth. Equally, I feel that we need to offer opportunities for children to develop digital skills to help them to understand the technology-rich world around them and to be empowered to actively engage with it. I believe that the primary computing curriculum offers these opportunities and I would also argue that its brevity provides space for this to be delivered in a range of ways that meet the needs of the individual, whilst stimulating and stretching them. The primary computing curriculum also offers a number of opportunities for cross-curricular working, reinforcing the concepts and reiterating the relevance of computing.

As with all times of transition, there are a range of responses to change. Concerns are often linked to the resources required and whether they are available or whether teachers have the confidence to deliver the new content. In an attempt to standardise and address a lack of confidence in the content, schemes of work and step-by-step worksheets are frequently developed. These often focus on a product rather than the learning that takes place through the process. Teachers should remember that they are experts in pedagogy and use this strength as they become increasingly confident with the curriculum content. This discussion will explore the pedagogy and theories that can help the coding novice to effectively deliver the primary computing curriculum content.

One major advantage of using an app developer program as one of the tools for teaching the primary computing curriculum is that you code an app that you can play on your mobile device, providing immediate relevancy and placing coding into a meaningful context. You also empower children to see themselves as makers and creators, rather than as passive consumers of other people's content. I have to confess that I find it very satisfying to be able to play a game, that I have created, on my phone.

## Computational thinking

Software such as *TouchDevelop* and others like *App Inventor* can be introduced in Key Stage 1 and 2 in the same way that you would introduce any other coding software, remembering that at this level these are best introduced in conjunction with a range of 'unplugged' activities that develop the key computing skills. There is a requirement that children have repeated opportunities and experiences of a number of programming languages (DfE, 2013) and the app developer languages can help to offer this. Introducing this sort of programming gives children an opportunity to become familiar with an environment that they may use independently later. I would suggest using an interactive whiteboard, where the teacher demonstrates the software to the whole class to encourage discussion. It would be useful to make links to other programming experiences that the children may have already had, so that they can start to identify similarities. This will help them to recognise the skills that can be transferred to other programming environments. You can demonstrate simple coding steps in *TouchDevelop* and the impact that these have on the environment and sprites. This will help the pupils to develop and reinforce an understanding of the following key concepts of computing:

- *Algorithms* are unambiguous sets of instructions for a specified outcome.

- *Decomposition* is a process of taking the problem apart to find a solution.

- *Debugging* is about working out why your algorithm is not achieving what you had anticipated and what you have to do to get the result that you need.

- *Abstraction* is where you remove the details so that you can focus on a few concepts at a time. A famous example of an abstraction is the London Tube map, which gives you sufficient detail so that you can make your journey without being distracted by details that you do not need, such as the actual distance between stations. Abstraction at this level can be achieved by using simple loops as demonstrated in the Turtle Challenge activity, which can also help to reinforce mathematical concepts such as the link between the number of sides of a shape and the angles.

- *Computational thinking* is a term developed in 2006 by Jeannette Wing. It is about not thinking like a computer; it is a process that considers problems and their solutions so that they can be carried out by a computer. It involves problem-solving, logic and algorithmic thinking, which is unambiguous step-by-step thinking to achieve a specific goal.

## Talk for learning

These processes require pupils to make predictions, which can be tested by running the program. If the program did not perform in the way that was expected, children need to go back to the code or algorithm to debug it using computational thinking to solve the problem. These are conversations that you can have with your pupils to help them to develop these skills and clarify their thinking. This concept of the role of language and 'conversations' being significant in the development of mental functions is at the heart of social-constructivism and the work of Vygotsky (1978), and informs our daily practice. You could arguably achieve all of this using other programming environments, however an app creator has the advantage of giving pupils the experience of coding that can be run on mobile devices, allowing them to create and share with their friends and family. As pupils make the transition into Key Stage 2 and beyond, the focus of activities will be on the pupils working more independently, whether that is alone or in groups to create their own apps, including the planning and developing process. Remember that the conversations continue to be important in the learning process and that you need to encourage pupils to verbalise their thinking processes in order to help them to remember and make sense of their work (Wegerif, 2013).

## Digital literacy

Mitch Resnick (2013) from MIT, one of the developers of *Scratch*, is one of the key proponents for making comparisons between reading skills or literacy and digital skills. He proposes that digital literacy is a key skill that individuals need to develop to become full citizens of a technology-rich society. Resnick proposes that children need to become fluent in these digital literacies, as using technology to play games, search the internet, communicate digitally, create digital products and write code is just as important as reading and writing. He suggests that there is no real expectation that every person who learns how to code will wish to end up programming as a career but that it is important that everyone understands the process. Experience of coding helps to develop logic, algorithmic thinking and problem solving; it also helps individuals develop persistence, a skill that is useful in all areas of life. The processes of debugging and persistence are particularly well-supported within *TouchDevelop*, through the simplicity of changing the code then running it to see its impact, the hints provided throughout the process and through possibly the most important feature, the desirability of the 'end product' being a playable game that you would be proud to share with others.

## The learner-led approach

The child-led, experiential learning approach that we have been discussing is often associated with coding environments such as *Scratch*, *Kodu* and *TouchDevelop*. However, it has its roots in the work of a number of theories from previous centuries. For example Froebel (1782–1852) introduced the concept of 'kindergarten', where children were provided with stimulating environments that were designed to develop their imagination and physical skills. Froebel developed a series of 'building gifts' consisting of blocks in different shapes and quantities and encouraged pre-school children to develop an understanding of the world around them through playing and observing their properties. It is not too much of a leap to see the blocks of visual coding in programs such as *Scratch*, *Hopscotch* and *TouchDevelop* as a virtual form of

Froebel's blocks, and similarly there is much to be gained from playful exploration of their properties. Indeed the developers of *Scratch* recognise that this concept is the foundation of their approach.

We have already suggested that the work of Vygotsky (1978) informs us about how we use conversations to help children to develop their understanding and that the discussions about prediction and the use of logic to make these predictions help to reinforce the concepts of coding. Dewey's (1902) work suggests that pupils should be proactive in these conversations and the learning activities, as he feels that the teacher should not be one to stand at the front of the room doling out bits of information to be absorbed by passive students. Instead, the teacher's role should be that of facilitator and guide. The programming environments we have discussed, and the availability of online tutorials that pupils can use for themselves, particularly facilitate this. This learner-led approach, where the teacher acts as the 'Sage on the side' encouraging children to work things out for themselves, is taken further by the work of Sugata Mitra, who is well known for his Hole in the Wall experiments (Mitra, 2010). Sugata Mitra placed computers into Indian slums, where children taught themselves to use the computers and in most cases how to read and speak English so that they could do this. Popular conception of Mitra's 'Self Organised Learning' work is that he was suggesting that there was no need for teachers. However, this work was looking at increasing educational opportunities (Mitra and Negroponte, 2012). What we can take from this and his continued work on Self-Organised Learning, which included a primary school in the north-east of England, is that encouraging children to seek out the answers for themselves, using the internet and their peers to solve their problems, creates a rich learning experience where they develop deep learning that is maintained, if not improved, when tested months later (Mitra *et al.*, 2010).

Creating apps that can be shared, in my opinion, is an example of authentic learning. App building creates a purpose for the activity beyond hitting the designated assessment criteria. Dewey's (1902) work on the power of authentic learning experiences recognised the need for children to interact with the curriculum whilst taking an active part in their own learning. He suggested that school is a place where children not only learn the curriculum, but they also learn how to become part of our society, and this should take account of students' interests. Building apps could be argued to be part of this process.

## The role of the teacher

Another approach that I find useful when teaching coding in primary schools also uses authenticity as its starting point and resonates with the work of both Mitra and Dewey; this is the work of maths teacher, Dan Meyer. Meyer's premise for teaching maths effectively to those who don't want to learn maths is 'Be less helpful'. He suggests that the examples in most maths textbooks are very wordy and that success is based on inserting values from examples into new questions, rather than learning the process. Meyer urges us to allow children to formulate the problem rather than the teacher providing a smooth and easy path to the solution. This is why I feel that there are risks in using step-by-step instructions and worksheets; success can be based on the ability to decode the worksheets rather than a knowledge of coding. You do need to create an environment where it is safe to take risks in terms of finding an answer so that children have to think, predict and have conversations to work out the solution. The real learning happens when children have to think hard, try things out and discuss strategies with each other. It is when they arrive at a solution that the 'wow' moments literally happen (Meyer, 2010). These wow moments not only improve motivation to persevere when things are difficult, they also help to reinforce the learning process and improve self-esteem.

## Connectivism

A number of coding programs, including *TouchDevelop*, *Scratch* and *Kodu* foster communities where you can share your projects so that others can play them and give feedback. Through this process of dialogue pupils begin to recognise that as knowledge changes, it is not just the knowledge itself that is important but knowing where and how to access knowledge or the individuals that hold that knowledge is also important. This process is recognised in Mitra's work and George Siemens' (2004) work on connectivism, which seeks to explain learning practices that are embedded in the use of technology, particularly the internet. Connectivism moves away from traditional learning theories by drawing on the theories of chaos, complexity, self-organisation and networking. It recognises that learning is messy and cannot be controlled by an individual. Rather, learning is dependent on connections and connectedness. With the advent of technology, knowledge can reside outside of the individual, for example within a database or a network, and understanding how to access this knowledge quickly is vital. Consequently, it is important to nurture and maintain learning networks, focusing in particular on the hubs that grant access to other networks.

## Assessment

Like other areas of the primary curriculum, the attainment targets for the computing curriculum are:

> *By the end of each key stage, pupils are expected to know, apply and understand the matters, skills and processes specified in the relevant programme of study.*

> (DfE, 2013)

This broad statement can seem daunting as you start to plan ways of recording progress. Computing at School (**www.computingatschool.org.uk**) has developed a progression pathway that can help you to identify what students should achieve. You could also use a mobile device to video children discussing the process of creating their apps. This raises the question of where you save all of this information so that can you share it and find it when you need to, particularly if you are working across platforms. I find programs such as *Evernote* (**https://evernote.com**) useful for this, as you can use it on a range of devices, and save files, photos and audio recordings. You can then use tags to sort the entries so that you can retrieve all entries for a particular child, group or type of activity. This makes it easier to share work with parents and colleagues.

---

## Summary and Key Points

In this chapter we have looked at using app building software to extend learning about computing and writing code, and how to use programming skills to build an app to play and share. We started by using the Turtle Challenge to introduce the *TouchDevelop* environment and made comparisons with other coding experiences. Building on these skills, we explored the use of *TouchDevelop* to build a simple game and considered the publishing options. As we worked through these examples, we explored ways of delivering these activities so that they covered a range of abilities and made cross-curricular links with maths. We then reflected on the pedagogy and theories that could inform the process of app creation, focusing on encouraging pupils to see themselves as makers and creators.

---

## Useful Links

http://youtu.be/adYPsk6J5Qw (accessed 20 December 2014).

*YouTube*

*TouchDevelop* – Follower Game Tutorial

Simple tutorial

http://youtu.be/UUq4Zc-o_20 (accessed 20 December 2014).

TouchDevelop – Lesson 1 – How to change a background on an application

One of a series

Ray Chambers @Lanky_Boi_Ray

Head of IT Uppingham Community College – Rutland regularly demonstrates for Microsoft at events such as BETT

Microsoft Innovative Education Expert

http://youtu.be/r_OuucF_MmY (accessed 20 December 2014).

*TouchDevelop* Curriculum – Activity 1a (Creating a new script)

One of a series

David Renton

@drenton72

Microsoft MPV (Most Valuable Professional) Lecturer in Games Development at West College Scotland

**http://youtu.be/r-D5wu-2Q6Q** (accessed 20 December 2014).

*TouchDevelop* Curriculum – Activity 1b (Creating a game script)

One of a series

David Renton

**http://youtu.be/Di0QwNPnsFI** (accessed 20 December 2014).

*TouchDevelop* Curriculum – Activity 2a (Create a Fruit Ninja Clone on a tablet)

One of a series

David Renton

**www.touchdevelop.com/hourofcode2** (accessed 20 December 2014).

*TouchDevelop* hour of code

Microsoft

A number of tutorials to support Hour of Code

**http://youtu.be/HbntNGGXamw?list=PLsxoqvm6HPQV5XMPwN4N0tYIe7asB81PS** (accessed 20 December 2014).

*App Inventor2*

One of a series

David Wolber

**appinventor.org**

This *App Inventor2* tutorial series takes light hearted approach

## App List for the Chapter

*TouchDevelop*

Microsoft

**www.touchdevelop.com** (accessed 20 December 2014).

Online free to use app creator

*App Inventor2*

MIT

**http://ai2.appinventor.mit.edu** (accessed 20 December 2014).

Online free to use app creator

*Kodu*

Microsoft

**www.kodugamelab.com** (accessed 20 December 2014).

Free to use visual programming software to create games using a PC or Xbox.

This is a simple to use program that creates games which can be used from Key Stage 1, but is probably more suitable for Key Stage 2 and above.

There are many tutorial videos available.

Online community to share projects.

Annual competition – the Kodu Kup.

*Scratch*

MIT

**http://scratch.mit.edu** (accessed 20 December 2014).

Online free to use visual programming software to create games, interactive stories and animations.

This is a simple to use versatile program that can be used from Key Stage 1 to adulthood.

There are many tutorial videos available.

Online community to share projects.

# Further Reading

Mitra, S and Negroponte, N (2012) *Beyond the Hole in the Wall: Discover the Power of Self-organised Learning.* Kindle Edition TED Books.

This book describes Mitra's work with the Hole in the Wall experiment and self-organised learning. Through this, he weaves a mythical story of a child that represents life and learning in a technology-rich future.

I like this book, as it explores learning and the impact that technology could have, resulting in some changes in roles as the learning environment is enriched.

I also like this book because it is an easy and quick read.

Renton, D (NA) *TouchDevelop Curriculum.* Available from: **https://az31353.vo.msecnd.net/cpd/uxvi-touchdevelopcurriculum.pdf** (accessed 20 December 2014).

This is a clear step by step guide to using *TouchDevelop* that could be used to supplement his videos.

Horspool, RN and Tillmann, N (2013) *TouchDevelop: Programming on the Go.* Apress. Available from: **www.touchdevelop.com/docs/book** (accessed 20 December 2014).

This is a free ebook that gives an in depth background to *TouchDevelop*. In my opinion this is really for the enthusiast and/or expert.

Belshaw, D (2014) *The Essential Elements of Digital Literacies.* Available from: **https://gumroad.com/l/digilit** (accessed 20 December 2014).

This is an online book that was released piecemeal, with readers providing feedback that informed future iterations; it is now complete.

What I like about this book in particular is the concept of the 8 Cs of digital literacy: cultural, communication, cognitive, citizenship, constructive, creativity, confidence, critical.

Computing at School. Available from: **www.computingatschool.org.uk** (accessed 20 December 2014).

Computing at School (CAS) aims to promote the teaching of computer science at school. Its goal is to put the excitement back into computing at school.

CAS is a grass-roots organisation, in collaboration with the BCS through the BCS Academy of Computing.

Membership is open to everyone, and is very broad, including teachers, parents, governors, exam boards, industry, professional societies and universities.

Joining the CAS community gives you access to a wide range of useful resources and support.

Computing Unplugged. Available from: **http://csunplugged.org** (accessed 20 December 2014).

CS Unplugged is a collection of free learning activities that teach computer science through engaging games and puzzles that use cards, string, crayons and lots of running around.

# References

Dewey, J (1902) *The Child and the Curriculum.* Chicago: University of Chicago Press.

DfE (2013) National curriculum in England: computing programmes of study.

Meyer, D (2010) Dan Meyer: Math class needs a makeover, in TED (ed.) *TED Talks.*

Mitra, S (2010) *Sugata Mitra: The Child-Driven Education.* Available from:**www.ted.com/talks/sugata_mitra_the_child_driven_education.html** (accessed 20 December 2014).

Mitra, S and Negroponte, N (2012) *Beyond the Hole in the Wall: Discover the Power of Self-organised Learning.* Kindle Edition TED Books.

Mitra, S, Leat, D, Dolan, P *et al.* (2010) The Self Organised Learning Environment (SOLE) School support pack, Technology AfL (ed).

Renton, D (NA) *TouchDevelop Curriculum.* Available from: **https://az31353.vo.msecnd.net/cpd/uxvi-touchdevelopcurriculum.pdf**

Resnick, M (2013) *Mitch Resnick: Let's Teach Kids to Code*, in TED (ed.) *TED Talks.*

Vygotsky, LS (1978) *Mind in Society: The Development of Higher Psychological Processes*. Cambridge, MA: Harvard University Press.

# Index